KERALA

A STATE STUDY GUIDE

AMBALI NAIR

Published by

Hawk Press
4836/24, Ansari Road, Daryaganj
New Delhi – 110 002
Phones: 91-11-23278618, 91-11-43667199
E-mail: thehawkpress@gmail.com
www.thehawkpress.com

ISBN: 978-93-88318-78-5

Preface

Kerala is a region where everything is dynamic. With its beautiful land, educated people and rich culture Kerala is unique in many ways. Kerala has been witnessing major changes since 1991 as a result of various structural adjustment programmes initiated by the Central and State Governments as a part of economic reforms.

Kerala is a state on the southwestern, Malabar Coast of India. It was formed on 1 November 1956 following the States Reorganisation Act by combining Malayalam-speaking regions. Spread over 38,863 km (15,005 sq mi), Kerala is the twenty second largest Indian state by area. It is bordered by Karnataka to the north and northeast, Tamil Nadu to the east and south, and the Lakshadweep Sea and Arabian Sea to the west. With 33,387,677 inhabitants as per the 2011 Census, Kerala is the thirteenth-largest Indian state by population. It is divided into 14 districts with the capital and largest city being Thiruvananthapuram. Malayalam is the most widely spoken language and is also the official language of the state.

The history of Kerala, India, dates back many millennia. Stone Age carvings in the Edakkal Caves feature pictorial writings believed to date to at least the Neolithic era around 5,000 BC, indicating the presence of a prehistoric civilisation or settlement in this region. From as early as 3000 BC, Chera nadu, currently known as Kerala had established itself as a major spice trade centre. Keralam, the then Chera nadu had direct contact across the Arabian Sea with all the major Mediterranean and Red Sea ports as well those of the Far East. The spice trade between Kerala and much of the world was one of the main drivers of the world economy. For much of history, ports in Kerala were the busiest (Muziris) among all trade and travel routes in the history of the world.

The culture of Kerala is a synthesis of Aryan and Dravidian cultures, developed and mixed for centuries, under influences from other parts of India and abroad. It is defined by its antiquity and the organic continuity sustained by the Malayali people. Modern Kerala society took shape owing to migrations from different parts of India and abroad throughout Classical Antiquity.

The Government of Kerala headquartered at Thiruvananthapuram is a democratically elected body that governs the Indian State of Kerala. The state government is headed by the Governor of Kerala as the nominal head of state, with a democratically elected Chief Minister as real head of the executive. The state government maintains its capital at Thiruvananthapuram (Trivandrum) and is seated at the Kerala Government Secretariat or the Hajur Kutcheri.

Politics in Kerala is dominated by two political fronts: the CPI(M)led Left Democratic Front (LDF) and the Indian National Congress-led United Democratic Front (UDF) since late 1970s. These two coalitions have alternated in power since 1982. According to the 2016 Kerala Legislative Assembly election, the LDF has a majority in the state assembly (92/140).

Kerala has the eight largest economy in India. Service industry dominates the Kerala economy. Kerala's per capita GDP in 2016-17 was Rs.140,107. Kerala's high GDP and productivity figures with higher development figures is often dubbed the "Kerala Phenomenon" or the "Kerala Model" of development by economists, political scientists, and sociologists.

This is a reference book. All the matter is just compiled and edited in nature, taken from the various sources which are in public domain.

This book provides a concise and lucid outline of the history of Kerala from the earliest period to the present, encompassing even the latest researches.

—Editor

ABOUT THE BOOK

Kerala is a region where everything is dynamic. With its beautiful land, educated people and rich culture Kerala is unique in many ways. Kerala has been witnessing major changes since 1991 as a result of various structural adjustment programmes initiated by the Central and State Governments as a part of economic reforms. Kerala is a state on the southwestern, Malabar Coast of India. It was formed on 1 November 1956 following the States Reorganisation Act by combining Malayalam-speaking regions. Spread over 38,863 km (15,005 sq mi), Kerala is the twenty second largest Indian state by area. It is bordered by Karnataka to the north and northeast, Tamil Nadu to the east and south, and the Lakshadweep Sea and Arabian Sea to the west. With 33,387,677 inhabitants as per the 2011 Census, Kerala is the thirteenth-largest Indian state by population. It is divided into 14 districts with the capital and largest city being Thiruvananthapuram. Malayalam is the most widely spoken language and is also the official language of the state. The culture of Kerala is a synthesis of Aryan and Dravidian cultures, developed and mixed for centuries, under influences from other parts of India and abroad. It is defined by its antiquity and the organic continuity sustained by the Malayali people. The Government of Kerala was formed on November 1, 1956 after merging of State of Travancore-Cochin with the Malabar district of the Madras state as part of States Reorganisation Act, 1956. Kerala has a unique position in India as one of the most politicised states. It has the nation's largest politically aware population, which actively participates in state politics. This book provides a concise and lucid outline of the history of Kerala from the earliest period to the present, encompassing even the latest researches.

Contents

1

State at a Glance

Kerala is a state on the southwestern, Malabar Coast of India. It was formed on 1 November 1956 following the States Reorganisation Act by combining Malayalam-speaking regions. Spread over 38,863 km (15,005 sq mi), Kerala is the twenty second largest Indian state by area. It is bordered by Karnataka to the north and northeast, Tamil Nadu to the east and south, and the Lakshadweep Sea and Arabian Sea to the west. With 33,387,677 inhabitants as per the 2011 Census, Kerala is the thirteenth-largest Indian state by population. It is divided into 14 districts with the capital and largest city being Thiruvananthapuram. Malayalam is the most widely spoken language and is also the official language of the state.

The Chera Dynasty was the first prominent kingdom based in Kerala. The Ay kingdom in the deep south and the Ezhimala kingdomin the north formed the other kingdoms in the early years of the Common Era (CE or AD). The region had been a prominent spice exporter since 3000 BCE. The region's prominence in trade was noted in the works of Pliny as well as the Periplus around 100 CE. In the 15th century, the spice trade attracted Portuguese traders to Kerala, and paved the way for European colonisation of India. At the time of Indian independence movement in the early 20th century, there were two major princely states in Kerala-Travancore State and the Kingdom of Cochin. They united to form the state of Thiru-Kochi in 1949. The Malabar region, in the northern part of

Kerala had been a part of the Madras province of British India, which later became a part of the Madras State post-independence.

After the States Reorganisation Act, 1956, the modern-day state of Kerala was formed by merging the Malabar district of Madras State (excluding Gudalur taluk of Nilgiris district, Topslip, the Attappadi Forest east of Anakatti), the state of Thiru-Kochi (excluding four southern taluks of Kanyakumari district, Shenkottai and Tenkasi taluks), and the taluk of Kasaragod (now Kasaragod District) in South Canara (Tulunad) which was a part of Madras State.

The economy of Kerala is the 12th-largest state economy in India with 7.73 lakh crore (US$110 billion) in gross domestic productand a per capita GDP of 163,000 (US$2,300). Kerala has the lowest positive population growth rate in India, 3.44%; the highest Human Development Index (HDI), 0.712 in 2015; the highest literacy rate, 93.91% in the 2011 census; the highest life expectancy, 77 years; and the highest sex ratio, 1,084 women per 1,000 men. The state has witnessed significant emigration, especially to Arab states of the Persian Gulf during the Gulf Boom of the 1970s and early 1980s, and its economy depends significantly on remittances from a large Malayali expatriate community. Hinduism is practised by more than half of the population, followed by Islam and Christianity. The culture is a synthesis of Aryan, Dravidian, Arab, and European cultures, developed over millennia, under influences from other parts of India and abroad.

The production of pepper and natural rubber contributes significantly to the total national output. In the agricultural sector, coconut, tea, coffee, cashew and spices are important. The state's coastline extends for 595 kilometres (370 mi), and around 1.1 million people in the state are dependent on the fishery industry which contributes 3% to the state's income. The state has the highest media exposure in India with newspapers publishing in nine languages, mainly English and Malayalam. Kerala is one of the prominent tourist destinations of India, with backwaters, hill stations, beaches, Ayurvedic tourism and tropical greenery as its major attractions.

ETYMOLOGY

The name Kerala has an uncertain etymology. One popular theory derives *Kerala* from *Kera* ("coconut tree" in Malayalam) and *alam*("land"); thus "land of coconuts", which is a nickname for the state, used by locals, due to abundance of coconut trees.

The word *Kerala* is first recorded as *Keralaputra* in a 3rd-century BCE rock inscription left by the Maurya emperor Ashoka (274–237 BCE), one of his edicts pertaining to welfare. The inscription refers to the local ruler as *Keralaputra* (Sanskrit for "son of Kerala"); or "son of Chera[s]".

This contradicts the theory that *Kera* is from "coconut tree". At that time, one of three states in the region was called *Cheralam* in Classical Tamil: *Chera* and *Kera* are variants of the same word. The word *Cheral* refers to the oldest known dynasty of Kerala kings and is derived from the Proto-Tamil-Malayalam word for "lake".

The earliest Sanskrit text to mention Kerala is the Aitareya Aranyaka of the Rigveda. Kerala is also mentioned in the Ramayana and the Mahabharata, the two Hindu epics.

The *Skanda Purana* mentions the ecclesiastical office of the Thachudaya Kaimal who is referred to as *Manikkam Keralar*, synonymous with the deity of the Koodalmanikyam temple.

Keralam may stem from the Classical Tamil *cherive-alam* ("declivity of a hill or a mountain slope") or *chera alam* ("Land of the Cheras"). The Greco-Romantrade map *Periplus Maris Erythraei* refers to Keralaputra as *Celobotra.*

HISTORY OF KERALA

The history of Kerala, India, dates back many millennia. Stone Age carvings in the Edakkal Caves feature pictorial writings believed to date to at least the Neolithic era around 5,000 BC, indicating the presence of a prehistoric civilisation or settlement in this region. From as early as 3000 BC, Chera nadu, currently known as Kerala had established itself as a major spice trade centre. Keralam, the then Chera nadu had direct contact across the Arabian Sea with all the major

Mediterranean and Red Sea ports as well those of the Far East. The spice trade between Kerala and much of the world was one of the main drivers of the world economy. For much of history, ports in Kerala were the busiest (Muziris) among all trade and travel routes in the history of the world.

The word *Kerala* is first recorded (as *Keralaputra*) in a 3rd-century BC rock inscription (Rock Edict 2) left by the Maurya emperor Ashoka (274–237 BC).

The Land of Keralaputra was one of the five independent kingdoms in southern India during Ashoka's time, the others being Chola, Pandya, Tamiraparani and Satiyaputra. A 3rd century CE, Brahmi inscription, found on Edakal cave, Ambukuthi hill, contained the word 'Chera' ('kadummipudha chera'), the earliest inscriptional evidence of the dynasty Chera.

The Cheras collapsed after repeated attacks from the neighboring Chola Empire and Rashtrakuta Empire. In the 8th century, Adi Shankara was born at Kalady in central Kerala. He travelled extensively across the Indian subcontinent establishing institutions of Advaita Vedanta philosophy.

Contact with Europeans after the arrival of Vasco Da Gama in 1498 gave rise to struggles between colonial and native interests. The state of Keralam was created in 1956 from the former state of Travancore-Cochin, the Malabar district of Madras State, and the Kasaragod taluk of Dakshina Kannada.

Mythology

According to Tamil classic *Purananuru*, Chera king Senkuttuvan conquered the lands between Kanyakumari and the Himalayas.Lacking worthy enemies, he besieged the sea by throwing his spear into it. According to the 17th century Malayalam work *Keralolpathi*, the lands of Kerala were recovered from the sea by the axe-wielding warrior sage Parasurama, the sixth avatar of Vishnu (hence, Kerala is also called *Parasurama Kshetram* ("The Land of Parasurama")). Parasurama threw his axe across the sea, and the water receded as far as it reached.

Parasurama, surrounded by settlers, commanding Varuna (the Hindu God of water) to part the seas and reveal Kerala

According to legend, this new area of land extended from Gokarna to Kanyakumari. The land which rose from sea was filled with salt and unsuitable for habitation; so Parasurama invoked the Snake King Vasuki, who spat holy poison and converted the soil into fertile lush green land. Out of respect, Vasuki and all snakes were appointed as protectors and guardians of the land. P. T. Srinivasa Iyengar theorised, that Senkuttuvan may have been inspired by the Parasurama legend, which was brought by early Aryan settlers.

Another much earlier Puranic character associated with Kerala is Mahabali, an Asura and a prototypical just king, who ruled the earth from Kerala. He won the war against the Devas, driving them into exile. The Devas pleaded before Lord *Vishnu*, who took his fifth incarnation as *Vamana* and pushed Mahabali down to Patala (the netherworld) to placate the Devas. There is a belief that, once a year during the Onamfestival, Mahabali returns to Kerala. The Matsya Purana, among the oldest of the 18 Puranas, uses the Malaya Mountains of Kerala (and Tamil Nadu) as the setting for the story of Matsya, the first incarnation of Vishnu, and Manu, the first man and the king of the region.

Pre-history

A dolmen erected by Neolithic people in Marayur

A substantial portion of Kerala may have been under the sea in ancient times. Marine fossils have been found in an area near Changanacherry, thus supporting the hypothesis. Pre-historical archaeological findings include dolmens of the Neolithic era in the Marayur area of the Idukki district. They are locally known as "muniyara", derived from *muni* (hermit or sage) and *ara* (dolmen). Rock engravings in the Edakkal Caves, in Wayanad date back to the Neolithic era around 6000 BCE. Archaeological studies have identified Mesolithic, Neolithic and Megalithic sites in Kerala. The studies point to the development of ancient Kerala society and its culture beginning from the Paleolithic Age, through the Mesolithic, Neolithic and Megalithic Ages. Foreign cultural contacts have assisted this cultural formation; historians suggest a possible relationship with Indus Valley Civilization during the late Bronze Age and early Iron Age.

Ancient period

Kerala has been a major spice exporter since 3000 BCE, according to Sumerian records and it is still referred to as the "Garden of Spices" or as the "Spice Garden of India". Kerala's spices attracted ancient Babylonians, Assyrians and Egyptians to the Malabar Coast in the 3rd and 2nd millennia BCE. Phoeniciansestablished trade with Kerala during this period. The *Land of Keralaputra* was one of the four independent kingdoms in southern India during Ashoka's time, the others being Chola, Pandya, and Satiyaputra. Scholars hold that Keralaputra is an alternate name of the Cheras, the first dominant dynasty based in Kerala. These territories once shared a common language and culture, within an area known as Tamilakam. Along with the Ay kingdom in the south and the Ezhimala kingdom in the north, the Cheras formed the ruling kingdoms of Kerala in the early years of the Common Era (CE). It is noted in Sangam literature that the Chera king Uthiyan Cheralathan ruled most of modern Kerala from his capital in Kuttanad, and controlled the port of Muziris, but its southern tip was in the kingdom of Pandyas, which had a trading port sometimes identified in ancient Western sources as *Nelcynda* (or *Neacyndi*) in Quilon. The lesser known Ays and Mushikas kingdoms lay to the south and north of the Chera regions respectively.

In the last centuries BCE the coast became important to the Greeks and Romans for its spices, especially black pepper. The Cheras had trading links with China, West Asia, Egypt, Greece, and the Roman Empire. In foreign-trade circles the region was known as *Male* or *Malabar*. Muziris, Berkarai, and Nelcynda were among the principal ports at that time. The value of Rome's annual trade with the region was estimated at around 50,000,000 sesterces; contemporary Sangam literature describes Roman ships coming to Muziris in Kerala, laden with gold to exchange for pepper. One of the earliest western traders to use the monsoon winds to reach Kerala was Eudoxus of

Cyzicus, around 118 or 166 BCE, under the patronage of Ptolemy VIII, king of the Hellenistic Ptolemaic dynasty in Egypt. Roman establishments in the port cities of the region, such as a temple of *Augustus* and barracks for garrisoned Roman soldiers, are marked in the Tabula Peutingeriana; the only surviving map of the Roman *cursus publicus.*

Merchants from West Asia and Southern Europe established coastal posts and settlements in Kerala. The Israeli (Jewish) connection with Kerala started in 573 BCE. Arabs also had trade links with Kerala, starting before the 4th century BCE, as Herodotus (484–413 BCE) noted that goods brought by Arabs from Kerala were sold to the Israelis [Hebrew (Jews)] at Eden. Israelis intermarried with local (Cheras Dravidian) people, resulting in formation of the Mappila community. In the 4th century, some Christians also migrated from Persia and joined the early Syriac Christian community who trace their origins to the evangelistic activity of Thomas the Apostle in the 1st century. *Mappila (Semitic)* was an honorific title that had been assigned to respected visitors from abroad; Israelite(Jewish), Syrian (Aramaic) Christian, and Muslim immigration account for later names of the respective communities: Juda Mappilas, Nasrani Mappilas, and Muslim Mappilas. The earliest Saint Thomas Christian Churches, Cheraman Juma Masjid (629 CE)—the first mosque of India—and Paradesi Synagogue (1568 CE)—the oldest active synagogue in the Commonwealth of Nations—were built in Kerala.

Early medieval period

A second Chera Kingdom (c. 800–1102), also known as Kulasekhara dynasty of Mahodayapuram (present-day Kodungallur), was established by Kulasekhara Varman, which ruled over a territory comprising the whole of modern Kerala and a smaller part of modern Tamil Nadu. During the early part of the Kulasekara period, the southern region from Nagercoil to Thiruvalla was ruled by Ay kings, who lost their power in the 10th century, making the region a part of the Kulasekara empire. Under Kulasekhara rule, Kerala witnessed a developing period of art, literature, trade and the Bhakti movement of Hinduism. A Keralite identity, distinct from the Tamils, became linguistically separate during this period around the seventh century. For local administration, the empire was divided into provinces under the rule of Naduvazhis, with each province comprising a number of *Desams* under the control of chieftains, called as *Desavazhis*.

The inhibitions, caused by a series of Chera-Chola wars in the 11th century, resulted in the decline of foreign trade in Kerala ports. In addition, Portuguese invasions in the 15th century caused two major religion Buddhism and Jainism to disappear from the land. It is known that the Menons in the Malabar region of Kerala were originally strong believers of Jainism. The social system became fractured with divisions on caste lines. Finally, the Kulasekhara dynasty was subjugated in 1102 by the combined attack of Later Pandyas and Later Cholas. However, in the 14th century, Ravi Varma Kulashekhara (1299–1314) of the southern Venad kingdom was able to establish a short-lived supremacy over southern India. After his death, in the absence of a strong central power, the state was divided into thirty small warring principalities; the most powerful of them were the kingdom of Samuthiri in the north, Venad in the south and Kochi in the middle. In the 18th Century, Travancore King Sree Anizham Thirunal Marthanda Varma annexed all the kingdoms up to Northern Kerala through military conquests, resulting in the rise of Travancore to pre-eminence in Kerala. The Kochi ruler sued for peace with Anizham Thirunal and Malabar came under direct British rule until India became independent.

Colonial era

The maritime spice trade monopoly in the Indian Ocean (Indu Maha Samundr) stayed with the Arabs during the High and Late Middle Ages. However, the dominance of Middle East traders was challenged in the European Age of Discovery. After Vasco Da Gama's arrival in Kappad Kozhikode in 1498, the Portuguese began to dominate eastern shipping, and the spice-trade in particular. The Zamorin of Kozhikode permitted the new visitors to trade with his subjects such that Portuguese trade in Kozhikode prospered with the establishment of a factory and a fort. However, Portuguese attacks on Arab properties in his jurisdiction provoked the Zamorin and led to conflicts between them. The Portuguese took advantage of the rivalry between the Zamorin and the King of Kochi allied with Kochi. When Francisco de Almeida was appointed as Viceroy of Portuguese India in 1505, his headquarters was established at Fort Kochi (Fort Emmanuel) rather than in Kozhikode. During his reign, the Portuguese managed to dominate relations with Kochi and established a few fortresses on the Malabar Coast. Fort St Angelo or St. Angelo Fort was built in 1505 by the Portuguese in Kannur. However, the Portuguese suffered setbacks from attacks by Zamorin forces; especially from naval attacks under the leadership Kozhikode admirals known as Kunjali Marakkars, which compelled them to seek a treaty. In 1571, the Portuguese were defeated by the Zamorin forces in the battle at Chaliyam fort.

The Portuguese were ousted by the Dutch East India Company, who during the conflicts between the Kozhikode and the Kochi, gained control of the trade. The Dutch in turn were weakened by constant battles with Marthanda Varma of the Travancore Royal Family, and were defeated at the Battle of Colachel in 1741. An agreement, known as "Treaty of Mavelikkara", was signed by the Dutch and Travancore in 1753, according to which the Dutch were compelled to detach from all political involvement in the region. Marthanda Varma annexed northern kingdoms through military conquests, resulting in the rise of Travancore to a position of preeminence in Kerala.

In 1766, Hyder Ali, the ruler of Mysore invaded northern Kerala. His son and successor, Tipu Sultan, launched campaigns against the expanding British East India Company, resulting in two of the four Anglo-Mysore Wars. Tipu ultimately ceded the Malabar District and South Kanara to the company in the 1790s; both were annexed to the Madras Presidency of British India in 1792. The company forged tributary alliances with Kochi in 1791 and Travancore in 1795. By the end of 18th century, the whole of Kerala fell under the control of the British, either administered directly or under suzerainty. There were major revolts in Kerala during the independence movement in the 20th century; most notable among them is the 1921 Malabar Rebellion and the social struggles in Travancore. In the Malabar Rebellion, Mappila Muslims of Malabar rioted against Hindu zamindars and the British Raj. Some social struggles against caste inequalities also erupted in the early decades of 20th century, leading to the 1936 Temple Entry Proclamation that opened Hindu temples in Travancore to all castes.

Post-colonial period

After India was partitioned in 1947 into India and Pakistan, Travancore and Kochi, part of the Union of India were merged on 1 July 1949 to form Travancore-Cochin. On 1 November 1956, the taluk of Kasargod in the South Kanara district of Madras, the Malabar district of Madras, and Travancore-Cochin, without four southern taluks (which joined Tamil Nadu), merged to form the state of Kerala under the States Reorganisation Act.

A Communist-led government under E. M. S. Namboodiripad resulted from the first elections for the new Kerala Legislative Assembly in 1957. It was one of the earliest elected Communist governments, after Communist success in the 1945 elections in the Republic of San Marino. His government helped distribute land and implement educational reforms.

Reference in Old testament

Many historians locate port cities Ophir and Tarshish mentioned in old testament in ancient Kerala. Poovar near Thiruvananthapuram is believed to be Ophir mentioned in old testament bible. Similarly Kollam, another ancient port city, is believed to be Tarshish.

Kerala in Hindu Purana

Many of the legends from native people in Kerala are common with the rest of India coming from the Puranas.

Mahabali

Perhaps the most famous festival of Kerala, Onam, is deeply

rooted in Kerala traditions. Onam is associated with the legendary king Mahabali, who according to the Hindu Puranas, ruled the Earth and several other planetary systems from Kerala. His entire kingdom was then a land of immense prosperity and happiness. However, he was granted rule over one of the netherworld (*Patala*) planets called Sutala, by *Vamana*, the fifth *Avatar* (earthly incarnation) of Lord *Vishnu*. Onam is celebrated in Kerala with respect to Maveli Thampuran of Mavelikkara and Thrikkakkarayappan.

Other texts

The oldest of all the Puranas, the Matsya Purana, sets the story of the Matsya Avatar (fish incarnation) of Lord Vishnu, in the Western ghat Mountains of old Tamilnadu, which lie in between Chera Nadu and chola and pandiyanadu. The earliest Sanskrit text to mention Kerala by name is the Aitareya Aranyaka of the Rigveda. It is also mentioned in both the Ramayana and the Mahabharata

Parasurama

There are legends dealing with the origins of Kerala geographically and culturally. One such legend is the retrieval of Kerala from the sea, by Parasurama, a warrior sage. It proclaims that Parasurama, an Avatar of Mahavishnu, threw his battle axe into the sea. As a result, the land of Kerala arose, and thus was reclaimed from the waters.

He was the sixth of the ten avatars (incarnations) of Vishnu. The word Parasu means 'axe' in Sanskrit and therefore the name Parasurama means 'Ram with Axe. In Treta yuga, Parasurama retrieved the land submerged under the ocean from Varuna - the God of the Oceans and Bhumidevi - Goddess of Earth. From Gokarnam he reached Kanyakumari and threw his axe northward across the ocean. The place where the axe landed was Kerala. It was 160 katam (an old measure) of land lying between Gokarnam and Kanyakumari. Puranas say that it was Parasurama who planted the Brahmins and Nayakas in 64 regions of Kerala from Chera and Pandya regions. According to the puranas, Kerala is also known as Parasurama Kshetram, i.e., 'The Land of Parasurama', as the land was reclaimed from sea by him.

Prehistory

A dolmen erected by Neolithic people in Marayur

Archaeological studies have identified many Mesolithic, Neolithic and Megalithic sites in Kerala. These findings have been classified into Laterite rock-cut caves (*Chenkallara*), Hood stones (*Kudakkallu*), Hat stones (*Toppikallu*), Dolmenoid cists (*Kalvrtham*), Urn burials (*Nannangadi*) and Menhirs (*Pulachikallu*). The studies point to the indigenous development of the ancient Kerala society and its culture beginning from the Paleolithic age, and its continuity through Mesolithic, Neolithic and Megalithic ages. However, foreign cultural contacts have assisted this cultural formation. The studies suggest possible relationship with Indus Valley Civilization during the late Bronze Age and early Iron Age.

Archaeological findings include dolmens of the Neolithic era in the Marayur area. They are locally known as "muniyara", derived from *muni*(hermit or sage) and *ara* (dolmen). Rock engravings in the Edakkal Caves in Wayanad are thought to date from the early to late Neolithic eras around 5000 BCE. Historian M.R. Raghava Varier of the Kerala state archaeology department identified a sign of "a man with jar cup" in the engravings, which is the most distinct motif of the Indus valley civilisation.

Ancient religions and ethnic groups

Buddhism and Jainism reached Kerala in this early period. As in other parts of Ancient India, Buddhism and Jainism co-existed with early Hindu beliefs during the first five centuries.

Merchants from West Asia and Southern Europe established coastal posts and settlements in Kerala. Jewish connection with Kerala started as early as 573 BC. Arabs also had trade links with Kerala, possibly started before the 4th century BC, as Herodotus (484–413 BC) noted that goods brought by Arabs from Kerala were sold to the Jews at Eden.In the 4th century, some Christians also immigrated from Persia and joined the early Syrian Christian community who trace their origins to the evangelistic activity of Thomas the Apostle in the 1st century. *Mappila* was an honorific title that had been assigned to respected visitors from abroad; and Jewish, Syrian Christian, and Muslim immigration might account for later names of the respective communities: Juda Mappilas, Nasrani Mappilas, and Muslim Mappilas. According to the legends of these communities, the earliest Christian churches, mosque, and synagogue(AD 1568) in India were built in Kerala. The combined number of Jews, Christians, and Muslims was relatively small at this early stage. They co-existed harmoniously with each other and with local Hindu society, aided by the commercial benefit from such association.

A silent revolution was taking place in the social system of the western coast of south India during the last phase of Sangam Age. Towards the end of Sangam age, Brahmins migrated into this region and by about the 8th century, a chain of Brahmin settlements had come up a large number of which were in Central Kerala. Temples were constructed, Nambudiri community was evolved. Adi Shankara the exponent of Advaita (monistic) philosophy lived in the 8th century AD. The whole of Kerala came to be covered by a network of Hindu temple centered Brahmin settlements. Under their control, these settlements had a large extend of land, number of tenants and the entailing privileges. With more advanced techniques of cultivation, sociopolitical organisation and a strong sense of solidarity, They succeeded in raising a feudal fighting class and ordered the caste system with numerous graduations of upper, intermediate and lower classes.

Early medieval period (c. 500-1400 CE)

Second Cheras

Much of history of the region from the 6th to the 8th century is obscure. A Second Chera Kingdom (c. 800–1102), also known as Kulasekhara dynasty of Mahodayapuram, was established by Kulasekhara Varman, which at its zenith ruled over a territory comprising the whole of modern Kerala and a smaller part of modern Tamil Nadu. During the early part of *Kulasekara period*, the southern region from Nagercoil to Thiruvananthapuram was ruled by Ay kings, who lost their power in 10th century and thus the region became a part of the*Kulasekara empire*. During Kulasekhara rule, Kerala witnessed a flourishing period of art, literatute, trade and the Bhakti movementof Hinduism. A Keralite identity, distinct from the Tamils, became linguistically separate during this period. For the local administration, the empire was divided into provinces under the rule of Nair Chieftains known as Naduvazhis, with each province comprising a number of *Desams* under the control of chieftains, called as *Desavazhis*.

The inhibitions, caused by a series of Chera-Chola wars in the 11th century, resulted in the decline of foreign trade in Kerala ports. Buddhism and Jainism disappeared from the land. The social system became fractured with internal divisions on the lines of caste. Finally, the Kulasekhara dynasty was subjugated in 1102 by the combined attack of *Later Pandyas* and Later Cholas. However, in the 14th century, Ravi Varma

Kulashekhara (1299-1314) of the southern Venad kingdom was able to establish a short-lived supremacy over southern India. After his death, in the absence of a strong central power, the state was fractured into about thirty small warring principalities under Nair Chieftains; most powerful of them were the kingdom of Samuthiri in the north, Venad in the south and Kochi in the middle.

Rise of Advaita

Adi Shankara (AD 789), one of the greatest Indian philosophers, was born in Kaladi in Kerala, and consolidated the doctrine of *advaita vedânta*. Shankara travelled across the Indian subcontinent to propagate his philosophy through discourses and debates with other thinkers. He is reputed to have founded four *mathas* ("monasteries"), which helped in the historical development, revival and spread of Advaita Vedanta of which he is known as the greatest revivalist. Adi Shankara is believed to be the organiser of the Dashanami monastic order and the founder of the Shanmatatradition of worship.

His works in Sanskrit concern themselves with establishing the doctrine of *advaita* (nondualism). He also established the importance of monastic life as sanctioned in the Upanishads and Brahma Sutra, in a time when the Mimamsa school established strict ritualism and ridiculed monasticism. Shankara represented his works as elaborating on ideas found in the *Upanishads*, and he wrote copious commentaries on the Vedic canon (*Brahma Sutra*, principal *upanishads* and *Bhagavad Gita*) in support of his thesis. The main opponent in his work is the Mimamsa school of thought, though he also offers arguments against the views of some other schools like Samkhya and certain schools of Buddhism.

Kingdom of Venad

Venad was a kingdom in the south west tip of Kerala, which acted as a buffer between Cheras and Pandyas. Until the end of the 11th century, it was a small principality in the Ay Kingdom. The *Ays* were the earliest ruling dynasty in southern Kerala, who, at their zenith, ruled over a region from Nagercoil in the south to Thiruvananthapuram in the north. Their capital was at Kollam. A series of attacks by the Pandyas between the 7th and 8th centuries caused the decline of Ays although the dynasty remained powerful until the beginning of the 10th century. When Ay power diminished, Venad became the southern most principality of the Second Chera Kingdom Invasion of Cholas into Venad caused the destruction of Kollam in 1096. However, the Chera capital, Mahodayapuram, fell in the subsequent attack, which compelled the Chera king, Rama varma Kulasekara, to shift his capital to Kollam. Thus, Rama Varma Kulasekara, the last emperor of Chera dynasty, is probably the founder of the Venad royal house, and the title of Chera kings, *Kulasekara*, was thenceforth adopted by the rulers of Venad. The end of Second Chera dynasty in the 12th century marks the independence of the Venad. The Venadu King then also was known as Venadu Mooppil Nayar.

In the second half of the 12th century, two branches of the Ay Dynasty: Thrippappur and Chirava, merged into the Venad family and established the tradition of designating the ruler of Venad as Chirava Moopan and the heir-apparent as *Thrippappur Moopan*. While Chrirava Moopan had his residence at Kollam, the Thrippappur Moopan resided at his palace in Thrippappur, 9 miles (14 km) north of Thiruvananthapuram, and was vested with the authority over the temples of Venad kingdom, especially the Sri Padmanabhaswamy temple.The most powerful kingdom of Kerala during the colonial period, Travancore, was developed through the expansion of Venad by Mahahrajah Marthanda Varma, a member of the Thrippappur branch of the Ay Dynasty who ascended to the throne in the 18th century.

Kingdom of Kozhikode

Historical records regarding the origin of the Samoothiri of Kozhikode is obscure. However, its generally agreed that the Samoothiri were originally the rulers of Eralnadu region of the Later Chera Kingdom and were known as the Eradis. Eralnadu province was situated in the northern parts of present-day Malappuram district and was landlocked by the Valluvanad and

Polanadu in the west. Legends such as *The Origin of Kerala* tell the establishment of a local ruling family at Nediyiruppu, near present-day Kondotty by two young brothers belonging to the Eradi clan. The brothers, Manikkan and Vikraman were the most trusted generals in the army of the Cheras. M.G.S. Narayanan, a Kerala-based historian, in his book, *Calicut: The City of Truth* states that the Eradi was a favourite of the last Later Chera king and granted him, as a mark of favor, a small tract of land on the sea-coast in addition to his hereditary possessions (Eralnadu province). Eradis subsequently moved their capital to the coastal marshy lands and established the kingdom of Kozhikode They later assumed the title of *Samudrâthiri* ("one who has the sea for his border") and continued to rule from Kozhikode.

Samoothiri allied with Muslim Arab and Chinese merchants and used most of the wealth from Kozhikode to develop his military power. They became the most powerful king in the Malayalam speaking regions during the Middle Ages. In the 14th century, Kozhikode conquered large parts of central Kerala, which was under the control of the king of Kingdom of Kochi. He was forced to shift his capital (c. AD 1405) further south. In the 15th century, Kochi was reduced in to a vassal state of Kozhikode .

Colonial period

The maritime spice trade monopoly in the Indian Ocean stayed with the Arabs during the High and Late Middle Ages. However, the dominance of Middle East traders was challenged in the European Age of Discovery. After Vasco Da Gama's arrival in Kappad Kozhikode in 1498, the Portuguesebegan to dominate eastern shipping, and the spice-trade in particular.

Portuguese period

The Samoothiri Maharaja of Kozhikode permitted the Portuguese to trade with his subjects. Their trade in Kozhikode prospered with the establishment of a factory and fort in his territory. However, Portuguese attacks on Arab properties in his jurisdiction provoked the Samoothiri and finally led to conflict.

The Portuguese took advantage of the rivalry between the Samoothiri and Rajah of Kochi—they allied with Kochi and when Francisco de Almeida was appointed Viceroy of Portuguese India in 1505, he established his headquarters at Kochi. During his reign, the Portuguese managed to dominate relations with Kochi and established a number of fortresses along the Malabar Coast. Nonetheless, the Portuguese suffered severe setbacks due to attacks by Samoothiri Maharaja's forces, especially naval attacks under the leadership of admirals of Kozhikode known as Kunjali Marakkars, which compelled them to seek a treaty. The Portuguese Cemetery, Kollam (after the invasion of Dutch, it became *Dutch Cemetery*) of Tangasseri in Kollam city was constructed in around 1519 as part of the Portuguese invasion in the city. Buckingham Canal(a small canal between Tangasseri Lighthouse and the cemetery) is situated very close to the Portuguese Cemetery. A group of pirates known as the Pirates of Tangasseri formerly lived at the Cemetery. The remnants of St. Thomas Fort and Portuguese Cemetery still exist at Tangasseri.

French Region in Kerala

The French East India Company constructed a fort on the site of Mahé in 1724, in accordance with an accord concluded between André Mollandin and Raja Vazhunnavar of Badagara three years earlier. In 1741, Mahé de La Bourdonnais retook the town after a period of occupation by the Marathas.

In 1761 the British captured Mahé, India, and the settlement was handed over to the Rajah of Kadathanadu. The British restored Mahé, India to the French as a part of the 1763 Treaty of Paris. In 1779, the Anglo-French war broke out, resulting in the French loss of Mahé, India. In 1783, the British agreed to restore to the French their settlements in India, and Mahé, India was handed over to the French in 1785

Dutch period

The weakened Portuguese were ousted by the Dutch East India Company, who took advantage of continuing conflicts between Kozhikodeand Kochi to gain control of the trade. The Dutch Malabar (1661-1795) in turn were weakened by their constant battles with Marthanda Varma of the Travancore Royal Family, and were defeated at the Battle of Colachel in 1741, resulting in the complete eclipse of Dutch power in Malabar. The Treaty of Mavelikkara was signed by the Dutch and Travancore in 1753, according to which the Dutch were compelled to detach from all political involvements in the region. In the meantime, Marthanda Varma annexed many smaller northern kingdoms through military conquests, resulting in the rise of Travancore to a position of preeminence in Kerala. Hyder Ali of Mysore conquered northern Kerala in the 18th century, capturing Kozhikode in 1766.

British period

Hyder Ali and his successor, Tipu Sultan, came into conflict with the British, leading to the four Anglo-Mysore wars fought across southern India in the latter half of the 18th century. Tipu Sultan ceded Malabar District to the British in 1792, and South Kanara, which included present-day Kasargod District, in 1799. The British concluded treaties of subsidiary alliance with the rulers of Cochin (1791) and Travancore (1795), and these became princely states of British India, maintaining local autonomy in return for a fixed annual tribute to the British. Malabar and South Kanara districts were part of British India's Madras Presidency.

Kerala Varma Pazhassi Raja (Kerul Varma Pyche Rajah, Cotiote Rajah) (3 January 1753 – 30 November 1805) was the Prince Regent and the de facto ruler of the Kingdom of Kottayam in Malabar, India between 1774 and 1805. He led the Pychy Rebellion (Wynaad Insurrection, Coiote War) against the English East India Company. He is popularly known as *Kerala Simham* (Lion of Kerala).

Organised expressions of discontent with British rule were not uncommon in Kerala. Uprisings of note include the rebellion by Pazhassi Raja, Velu Thampi Dalawa and the Punnapra-Vayalar revolt of 1946. In 1919, consequent to their victory in World War I, the British abolished the Islamic Caliphate and dismembered the Ottoman Empire. This resulted in protests against the British by Muslims of the Indian sub-continent known as the Khilafat Movement, which was supported by Mahatma Gandhi in order to draw the Muslims into the mainstream national independence movement. In 1921, the Khilafat Movement in Malabar culminated in widespread riots against the British government and Hindu population in what is now known as the Moplah rebellion. Kerala also witnessed several social reforms movements directed at the eradication of social evils such as untouchability among the Hindus, pioneered by reformists like Srinarayana guru and Chattambiswami among others. The non-violent and largely peaceful Vaikom Satyagraha of 1924 was instrumental in securing entry to the public roads adjacent to the Vaikom temple for people belonging to untouchable castes. In 1936, Sree Chithira Thirunal Balaramavarma, the ruler of Travancore, issued the Temple Entry Proclamation, declaring the temples of his kingdom open to all Hindu worshipers, irrespective of caste.

Modern history

Formation of Kerala state

The two independent kingdoms of Travancore and Cochin joined the Union of India after India gained independence in 1947. On 1 July 1949, the two states were merged to form Travancore-Cochin. On 1 January 1950, Travancore-Cochin was recognised as a state. The Madras Presidency was reorganised to form Madras State in 1947.

On 1 November 1956, the state of Kerala was formed by the States Reorganisation Act merging the Malabar district, Travancore-Cochin (excluding four southern taluks, which were merged with Tamil Nadu), and the taluk of Kasargod, South Kanara. In 1957, elections for the new Kerala Legislative Assembly were held, and a reformist, Communist-led government came to power, under E. M. S. Namboodiripad. It was the first time a Communist government was democratically elected to power anywhere in the world. It initiated pioneering land reforms, leading to lowest levels of rural poverty in India.

Liberation struggle

It refused to nationalise the large estates but did provide reforms to protect manual labourers and farm workers, and invited capitalists to set up industry. Much more controversial was an effort to impose state control on private schools, such as those run by the Christians and the Nairs, which enrolled 40% of the students. The Christians, the land owning communities of Nairs and Namputhiris and the Congress Party protested, with demonstrations numbering in the tens and hundreds of thousands of people. The government controlled the police, which made 150,000 arrests (often the same people arrested time and again), and used 248 lathi charges to beat back the demonstrators, killing twenty. The opposition called on Prime Minister Jawaharlal Nehru to seize control of the state government. Nehru was reluctant but when his daughter Indira Gandhi, the national head of the Congress Party, joined in, he finally did so. New elections in 1959 cost the Communists most of their seats and Congress resumed control.

Coalition politics

Later in 1967-82 Kerala elected a series of leftist coalition governments; the most stable was that led by Achutha Menon from 1969 to 1977.

From 1967 to 1970, Kunnikkal Narayanan led a Naxalite movement in Kerala. The theoretical difference in the communist party, i.e. CPM is the part of the uprising of Naxalbari movement in Bengal which leads to the formation of CPI(ML) in India.Due to the several difference in the ideological level the CPI-ML split into several groups. Some are come to the democratic way and some to the extreme, anarchic way. The violence alienated public opinion.

The political alliance have strongly stabilised in such a manner that, with rare exceptions, most of the coalition partners stick their loyalty to the alliance. As a result, to this, ever since 1979, the power has been clearly alternating between these two fronts without any change. Politics in Kerala is characterised by continually shifting alliances, party mergers and splits, factionalism within the coalitions and within political parties, and numerous splinter groups.

Modern politics in Kerala is dominated by two political fronts: the Communist party-led Left Democratic Front (LDF) and the Indian National Congress-led United Democratic Front(UDF) since the late 1970s. These two parties have alternating in power since 1982. Most of the major political parties in Kerala, except for Bharatiya Janata Party (BJP), belong to one or the other of these two alliances, often shifting allegiances a number of time. According to 2016 Kerala Legislative Assembly election results, the LDF has a majority in the state assembly seats (91/140)

MEDIA

The media, telecommunications, broadcasting and cable services are regulated by the Telecom Regulatory Authority of India (TRAI). The National Family Health Survey – 3, conducted in 2007, ranked Kerala as the state with the highest media exposure in India. Dozens of newspapers are published in Kerala, in nine major languages, but principally Malayalam and English. The most widely circulated Malayalam-language newspapers are *Malayala Manorama, Mathrubhumi, Madhyamam, Deshabhimani, Mangalam, Kerala Kaumudi, Chandrika, Thejas, Janayugam, Janmabhumi, Deepika* and *Siraj Daily*. Major Malayalam periodicals include *Mathrubhumi, India Today Malayalam, Madhyamam Weekly, Grihalakshmi, Vanitha, Dhanam, Chithrabhumi*, and *Bhashaposhini. The Hindu* is the most read English language newspaper in the state, followed by *The New Indian Express.*Other dailies include *Deccan Chronicle, The Times of India, DNA, The Economic Times*, and *The Financial Express.*

Doordarshan is the state-owned television broadcaster. Multi system operators provide a mix of Malayalam, English and international channels via cable television. Some of the popular Malayalam television channels are Asianet, Asianet News, Asianet Plus, Asianet Movies, Surya TV, Kiran TV, Mazhavil Manorama, Manorama News, Indiavision, Kairali TV, Kairali WE, Kairali People, Flowers, Yes Indiavision, Kappa TV, Amrita TV, Reporter,

Jaihind, Jeevan TV, Mathrubhumi News, Kaumudi, Shalom TV, and Janam TV. Television serials, reality shows and the Internet have become major sources of entertainment and information for the people of Kerala.

Malayala Manorama new office in Kottiyam, Kollam

A Malayalam version of Google News was launched in September 2008. A sizeable "people's science" movement has taken root in the state, and such activities as writers' cooperatives are becoming increasingly common. BSNL, Reliance Infocomm, Airtel, Vodafone, Idea, Jio, Tata Docomoand Aircel are the major cell phone service providers. Broadband Internet services are widely available throughout the state; some of the major ISPs are BSNL, Asianet Satellite communications, Reliance Communications, Airtel, Idea, MTS and VSNL. According to a TRAI report, as of January 2012 the total number of wireless phone subscribers in Kerala is about 34.3 million and the wireline subscriber base is at 3.2 million, accounting for the telephone density of 107.77. Unlike in many other states, the urban-rural divide is not visible in Kerala with respect to mobile phone penetration.

SPORTS

The annual snake boat race is performed during Onam on the Pamba River

By the 21st century, almost all of the native sports and games from Kerala have either disappeared or become just an art form performed during local festivals; including Poorakkali, Padayani, Thalappandukali, Onathallu, Parichamuttukali, Velakali, and Kilithattukali. However, *Kalaripayattu*, regarded as "the mother of all martial arts in the world", is an exception and is practised as the indigenous martial sport.Another traditional sport of Kerala is the boat race, especially the race of Snake boats.

Cricket and football became popular in the state; both were introduced in Malabar during the British colonial period in the 19th century. Cricketers, like Tinu Yohannan, Abey Kuruvilla, Sreesanth, Sanju Samson and Basil Thampi found places in the national cricket team. A cricket club from Kerala, the Kochi Tuskers, played in the Indian Premier League's fourth season. However, the team was disbanded after the season because of conflicts of interest among its franchises. Kerala has only performed well recently in the Ranji Trophy cricket competition, in 2017–18 reaching the quarterfinals for the first time in history. Football is one of the most widely played and watched sports with huge support for club and district level matches. Kochi hosts Kerala Blasters FC in the Indian Super League and Kozhikode hosts Gokulam Kerala FC in the I-League. Kozhikode also hosts the Sait Nagjee Football Tournament. Kerala is one of the major footballing states in India along with West Bengal and Goa and has produced national players like I. M. Vijayan, C. V. Pappachan, V. P. Sathyan, Jo Paul Ancheri, Pappachen Pradeep, Mohammed Rafi, C.K. Vineeth, Anas Edathodika and Rino Anto. The Kerala state football team has won the Santhosh Trophy six times; in 1973, 1992, 1993, 2001, 2004, and 2018. They were also the runners-up eight times.

Among the prominent athletes hailing from the state are P. T. Usha, Shiny Wilson and M.D. Valsamma, all three of whom are recipients of the Padma Shri as well as Arjuna Award, while K. M. Beenamol and Anju Bobby George are Rajiv Gandhi Khel Ratna and Arjuna Award winners. T. C. Yohannan, Suresh Babu, Sinimol Paulose, Angel Mary Joseph, Mercy Kuttan, K. Saramma, K. C. Rosakutty and Padmini Selvan are the other Arjuna Award winners from Kerala. Volleyball is another popular sport and is often played on makeshift courts on sandy beaches along the coast. Jimmy George was a notable Indian volleyball player, rated in his prime as among the world's ten best players. Other popular sports include badminton, basketball and kabaddi. The Indian Hockey team captain P. R. Shreejesh, ace goalkeeper hails from Kerala.

For the 2017 FIFA U-17 World Cup in India, the Jawaharlal Nehru Stadium (Kochi), was chosen as one of the six venues where the game would be hosted in India.

2

Culture and Society

CULTURE OF KERALA

The culture of Kerala is a synthesis of Aryan and Dravidian cultures, developed and mixed for centuries, under influences from other parts of India and abroad. It is defined by its antiquity and the organic continuity sustained by the Malayali people. Modern Kerala society took shape owing to migrations from different parts of India and abroad throughout Classical Antiquity.

Kerala traces its non-prehistoric cultural genesis to its membership (around the AD 3rd century) in a vaguely defined historical region known as *Thamizhagom* — a land defined by a common Tamil culture and encompassing the Chera, Chola, and Pandya kingdoms. At that time, the music, dance, language (first *Dravida Bhasha* — "Dravidian language" — then Tamil), and *Sangam* (a vast corpus of Tamil literature composed between 1,500–2,000 years ago) found in Kerala were all similar to that found in the rest of *Thamizhagom* (today's Tamil Nadu). The culture of Kerala evolved through the Sanskritization of Dravidian ethos, revivalism of religious movements and reform movementsagainst caste discrimination. Kerala showcases a culture unique to itself developed through accommodation, acculturation and assimilation of various faculties of civilized lifestyle.

Culture

A Kathakali artist

Theyyam, The ritual art of North Malabar

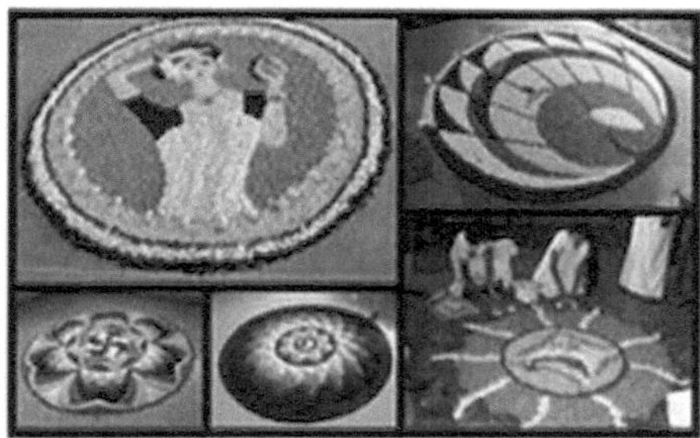

During Onam, Kerala's biggest celebration, Keralites create pookkalam *(floral carpet) designs in front of their houses.*

Thrissur Pooram festival

A mohiniattam *performance*

Thunchaththu Ramanujan Ezhuthachan, 17-century poet

Onam Sadya

The culture of Kerala is composite and cosmopolitan in nature and it is an integral part of Indian culture. It is synthesis of Aryan and Dravidian cultures, defined by its antiquity and the organic continuity sustained by the Malayali people. It has been elaborated through centuries of contact with neighbouring and overseas cultures.

However, the geographical insularity of Kerala from the rest of the country has resulted in the development of a distinctive lifestyle, art, architecture, language, literature and social institutions. Over 10,000 festivals are celebrated in the state every year. The Malayalam calendar, a solar calendar started from 825 CE in Kerala, finds common usage in planning agricultural and religious activities.

Festivals

Many of the temples in Kerala hold festivals on specific days of the year. A common characteristic of these festivals is the hoisting of a holy flag which is brought down on the final day of the festival after immersing the deity. Some festivals include Poorams, the best known of these being the Thrissur Pooram. "Elephants, firework displays and huge crowds" are the major attractions of Thrissur Pooram.Other known festivals are Makaravilakku, Chinakkathoor Pooram Nenmara Vallangi Vela and Utsavam. Temples that can afford it will usually involve at least one richly caparisoned elephant as part of the festivities. The idol in the temple is taken out on a procession around the countryside atop this elephant. When the procession visits homes around the temple, people will usually present rice, coconuts, and other offerings to it. Processions often include traditional music such as Panchari melam or Panchavadyam.

Onam

Onam is a harvest festival celebrated by the people of Kerala and is reminiscent of the state's agrarian past. It is a local festival of Kerala consisting of a four-day public holidays; from Onam Eve (Uthradam) to the fourth Onam Day. Onam falls in the Malayalam month of Chingam (August–September) and marks the commemoration of the Vamana avatara of Vishnu and the subsequent homecoming of King Mahabali. It is one of the festivals celebrated with cultural elements such as Vallam Kali, Pulikali,Pookkalam, Thumbi Thullal and Onavillu.

Dance

Kerala is home to a number of performance arts. These include five classical dance forms: Kathakali, Mohiniyattam, Koodiyattom, Thullaland Krishnanattam, which originated and developed in the temple theatres during the classical period under the patronage of royal houses. Kerala natanam,

Thirayattam, Kaliyattam, Theyyam, Koothu and Padayani are other dance forms associated with the temple culture of the region. Some traditional dance forms such as Margamkali and Parichamuttukali are popular among the Syrian Christians and Chavittu nadakom is popular among the Latin Christians, while Oppana and Duffmuttu are popular among the Muslims of the state.

Music

The development of classical music in Kerala is attributed to the contributions it received from the traditional performance arts associated with the temple culture of Kerala. The development of the indigenous classical music form, Sopana Sangeetham, illustrates the rich contribution that temple culture has made to the arts of Kerala. Carnatic music dominates Keralite traditional music. This was the result of Swathi Thirunal Rama Varma's popularisation of the genre in the 19th century. Raga-based renditions known as *sopanam* accompany *kathakali* performances. *Melam*; including the *paandi* and *panchari* variants, is a more percussive style of music: it is performed at *Kshetram*-centered festivals using the *chenda*. *Panchavadyam* is a form of percussion ensemble, in which artists use five types of percussion instrument. Kerala's visual arts range from traditional murals to the works of Raja Ravi Varma, the state's most renowned painter. Most of the castes and communities in Kerala have rich collections of folk songs and ballads associated with a variety of themes; *Vadakkan Pattukal* (Northern Ballads), *Thekkan pattukal* (Southern Ballads), *Vanchi pattukal* (Boat Songs), *Mappila Pattukal* (Muslim songs) and *Pallipattukal* (Church songs) are a few of them.

Cinema

Malayalam films carved a niche for themselves in the Indian film industry with the presentation of social themes. Directors from Kerala, like Adoor Gopalakrishnan, G. Aravindan, Bharathan, P. Padmarajan, M.T.Vasudevan Nair, K.G. George, Priyadarshan, John Abraham, Ramu Karyat, K S

Sethumadhavan, A. Vincent and Shaji N Karun have made a considerable contribution to the Indian parallel cinema. Kerala has also given birth to numerous actors, such as Satyan, Prem Nazir, Madhu, Sheela, Sharada, Miss Kumari, Jayan, Adoor Bhasi, Seema, Bharath Gopi, Thilakan, Mammootty, Mohanlal, Dileep, Shobana, Nivin Pauly, Sreenivasan, Urvashi, Manju Warrier,Suresh Gopi, Jayaram, Murali, Shankaradi, Kavya Madhavan, Prithviraj, Parvathy (actress), Jayasurya, Dulquer Salmaan, Tovino Thomas, Oduvil Unnikrishnan, Jagathy Sreekumar, Nedumudi Venu, KPAC Lalitha, Fahad Fazil and Asif Ali. Late Malayalam actor Prem Nazir holds the world record for having acted as the protagonist of over 720 movies. Since the 1980s, actors Mammootty and Mohanlal have dominated the movie industry; Mammootty has won three National Awards for best actor while Mohanlal has two to his credit. Malayalam Cinema has produced a few more notable personalities such as K.J. Yesudas, K.S. Chitra, Vayalar Rama Varma, M.T. Vasudevan Nair and O.N.V. Kurup, the last two mentioned being recipients of Jnanpith award, the highest literary award in India.

PERFORMING ARTS

Native traditions of classical performing arts include *koodiyattom*, a form of Sanskrit drama or theatre and a UNESCO-designated Human Heritage Art. Kathakali (from *katerumbu* ("story") and *kali* ("performance")) is a 500-year-old form of dance-drama that interprets ancient epics; a popularized offshoot of *kathakali* is *Kerala natanam* (developed in the 20th century by dancer Guru Gopinath). Meanwhile, *koothu* is a more light-hearted performance mode, akin to modern stand-up comedy; an ancient art originally confined to temple sanctuaries, it was later popularized by Mani Madhava Chakyar. Other Keralite performing arts include *mohiniyaattam* ("dance of the enchantress"), which is a type of graceful choreographed dance performed by women and accompanied by musical vocalizations. *Thullal*, *Thirayattam*, *padayani*, and *theyyam* are other important Keralite performing arts.Thirayattam is one of the most outstanding Ethnic art of kerala. This vibrant ritualistic annual performing art form enacted in courtyards of "Kaavukal"(sacred groves) and village shrine.

Kerala also has several tribal and folk art forms. For example, Kummattikali is the famous colorful mask-dance of South Malabar, performed during the festival of Onam. The Kannyar Kali dances (also known as Desathukali) are fast moving, militant dances attuned to rhythmic devotional folk songs and asuravadyas. Also important are various performance genres that are Islam- or Christianity-themed. These include *oppana*, which is widely popular among Keralite Muslims and is native to Malabar. *Oppana* incorporates group dance accompanied by the beat of rhythmic hand clapping and *ishal* vocalizations.

Margam Kali is one of the ancient round group dance of Kerala practiced by Saint Thomas Christians.

However, many of these native art forms largely play to tourists or at youth festivals, and are not as popular among ordinary Keralites. Thus, more contemporary forms — including those heavily based on the use of often risqué and politically incorrect mimicry and parody — have gained considerable mass appeal in recent years. Indeed, contemporary artists often use such modes to mock socioeconomic elites. In recent decades, Malayalam cinema, yet another mode of widely popular artistic expression, have provided a distinct and indigenous Keralite alternative to both Bollywood and Hollywood.

MUSIC

The *ragas* and *talas* of lyrical and devotional Carnatic music — another native product of South India — dominates Keralite classical musical genres. Swathi Thirunal Rama Varma, a 19th-century king of Travancore and patron and composer of music, was instrumental in popularising carnatic music in early Kerala. Additionally, Kerala has its own native music system, *sopanam*, which is a lugubrious and step-by-step rendition of raga-based songs. It is *Sopanam*, for example, that provides the background music used in *Kathakali*. The wider traditional music of Kerala also includes *melam* (including the *paandi* and *panchari* variants), as style of percussive music performed at temple-centered festivals using an instrument known as the *chenda*. Up to 150 musicians may comprise the ensembles staging a given performance; each performance, in turn, may last up to four hours. *Panchavadyam* is a differing type of percussion ensemble consisting of five types of percussion instruments; these can be utilised by up to one hundred artists in certain major festivals. In addition to these, percussive music is also associated with various uniquely Keralite folk arts forms. Lastly, the popular music of Kerala — as in the rest of India — is dominated by the *filmi* music of Indian cinema. The most remembered name in kerala music culture is of Great Indian musician Sri K. J. Yesudas.

FOLKLORE

Thirayattam(Pookkutty Thira)

The folklore of Kerala includes elements from the traditional lifestyle of the people of Kerala. The traditional beliefs, customs,rituals etc. are reflected in the folkart and songs of Kerala. Kerala has a rich tradition of Folklore. Folklore in this region is a spontaneous expression of human behavior and thoughts. Generally speaking, Folklore could be defined as the lore of the common people who had been marginalized during the reign of feudal Kings. The Keralites have their culture and lore which were mostly part of agricultural. Sowing, planting of nharu (seedling), clearing out the weeds, harvests etc. are the different stages of agriculture which have their typical rituals. Numerous songs and performing arts are accompanied with them. Kanyar Kali, Padayani, Mudiyettu, Thirayattam, Malavayiyattam, Theyyam, Kothamooriyattam, Nira, Puthari, etc. are some of the ritual folklore of Kerala. It was under the rule of Kolathiris, the Kings of Kolathunadu, and they codified the rituals, beliefs, taboos and folk performing arts. Even the dates of specific fertility rituals and folk performances were decided by the Kolathiris of which many are continuing even today.The Theyyam festivals, even now, are conducted as per the dates once fixed by the King.

The folk arts of Kerala can be broadly classified under two heads: ritualistic and non-ritualistic. Ritualistic folk arts can be further divided into two: devotional and magical. Devotional folk arts are performed to propitiate a particular God or Goddess. Theyyam, thirayattam, poothamthira, kanyarkali, kummatti, etc., are some of them. Forms like panappattu and thottampattu are composed in the form of songs. In kolkali, margamkali, daffumuttukkali, etc., the ritualistic element is not very strong. Magical folk arts seek to win general prosperity for a community or exorcise evil spirits or to beget children. Gandharvas and nagas are worshipped in order to win these favours. The magical folk arts include pambinthullal, pooppadathullal, kolamthullal, malayankettu, etc.

Onam

Onam is a harvest festival celebrated extravagantly by the people of Kerala, India. It is also the state festival of Kerala with State holidays on 4 days starting from Onam Eve (Uthradom) to the 4th Onam Day. Onam Festival falls during the Malayalam month of Chingam (Aug - Sep) and marks the commemoration of Vamana avatara of Vishnu and the subsequent homecoming of King Mahabali, who Malayalees consider to be just and fair King who was exiled to the underworld. Onam is reminiscent of Kerala's agrarian past, as it is considered to be a harvest festival. It is one of the festivals celebrated with most number of cultural elements. Some of them are Vallam Kali, Pulikkali, Pookkalam, Onatthappan, Thumbi Thullal, Onavillu, Kazhchakkula, Onapottan, Atthachamayame etc.

Another distinct feature of the festival is 'Ona Sadhya' (Onam Feast) and consists of numerous dishes served on banana leaf and 'Ona Kodi' (new dress for the special occasion). Usual the Ona Sadhya consist of numerous side dishes along with rice and Ona Kodi is traditional dress. Both are eagerly observed by the youth with excitement.

Politics

The people of Kerala are very fond of politics. Majority of keralites belong to either one of the political alliances namely United Democratic Front (UDF) or Left Democratic Front(LDF). Bharatiya Janatha Party (BJP), a national party, also has good following. Regional parties such as Indian Union Muslim League (IUML), various factions of Kerala Congress, various factions of Revolutionary Socialist Party and a host of smaller parties add spice to Kerala political scene. Religious leaders have high influence in Kerala political movements. For many Keralites it's nostalgic to remember the political discussions and debates they had done in the '*chaya kada*' (local tea shops were youngsters go to sip a cup and read newspapers) in their younger ages.

CUISINE OF KERALA

The cuisine of Kerala, a state in the south of India, is linked to its history, geography, demography and culture. Kerala cuisine offers a multitude of both vegetarian and non-vegetarian dishes prepared using fish, poultry and red meat with rice a typical accompaniment. Chillies, curry leaves, coconut, mustard seeds, turmeric, tamarind, and asafoetida are all frequently used.

Kerala is known as the "Land of Spices" because it traded spices with Europe as well as with many ancient civilizations with the oldest historical records of the Sumerians from 3000 BCE.

Kerala cuisine has a multitude of both vegetarian and non-vegetarian dishes prepared using fish, poultry, and meat. Culinary spices have been cultivated in Kerala for millennia and they are characteristic of its cuisine. Rice is a dominant staple that is eaten at all times of day. A majority of the breakfast foods in Kerala are made out of rice, in one form or the other (*idli*, *puttu*, *appam*, or *idiyappam*), tapioca preparations, or pulse-based vada. These may be accompanied by chutney, *kadala*, *payasam*, *payar pappadam*, *appam*, chicken curry, beef fry, egg masala and fish curry. Lunch dishes include rice and curry along with *rasam*, *pulisherry* and *sambar*. *Sadhya* is a vegetarian meal, which is served on a banana leaf and followed with a cup of payasam. Popular snacks include banana chips, yam crisps, tapioca chips, *unniyappam* and *kuzhalappam*. Seafood specialties include karimeen, prawns, shrimp and other crustacean dishes.

Elephants

Elephants have been an integral part of the culture of the state. Almost all of the local festivals in kerala include at least one richly caparisoned elephant. Kerala is home to the largest domesticated population of elephants in India—about 700 Indian elephants, owned by temples as well as individuals. These elephants are mainly employed for the processions and displays associated with festivals celebrated all around the state. More than 10,000 festivals are celebrated in the state annually and some animal lovers have sometimes raised concerns regarding the overwork of domesticated elephants during them. In Malayalam literature, elephants are referred to as the 'sons of the *sahya*. The elephant is the state animal of Kerala and is featured on the emblem of the Government of Kerala.

Historical and cultural influences

In addition to historical diversity, cultural influences, particularly the large percentages of Muslims and Christians, have also contributed unique dishes and styles to Kerala cuisine, especially non-vegetarian dishes. The meat eating habits of the people were historically limited by religious taboos. Brahmins eschew non vegetarian items. However, most modern-day Hindus do not observe any dietary taboos, except a few of those belonging to upper castes who do not consume beef or pork. Most Muslims do not eat pork and other items forbidden by Islamic law. Alcohol is available in Kerala in many hotels and over a thousand bars and liquor stores, but state authorities plan to close the vast majority of these outlets in a ten-year plan, beginning in 2014, to combat problem drinking.

Overview

One of the traditional Kerala dishes is vegetarian and is called the Kerala Sadya, which is an elaborate banquet prepared for festivals and ceremonies. A full-course Sadya, which consists of rice with about twenty different accompaniments and desserts is the ceremonial meal of Kerala eaten usually on celebratory occasions including marriages, Onam and Vishu. It is served on a plantain leaf.

Because of its rich trading heritage, over time various cuisines have blended with indigenous Kerala dishes with foreign dishes adapted to local tastes. Coconuts grow in abundance in Kerala, so grated coconut and coconut milk are commonly used for thickening and flavouring. Kerala's long coastline and numerous rivers have led to a strong fishing industry in the region, making seafood a common part of meals. Rice is grown in abundance along with tapioca. It is the main starch ingredient used in Kerala's food.

Having been a major production area of spices for thousands of years, the region makes frequent use of black pepper, cardamom, clove, ginger, and cinnamon. Kerala also has a variety of breakfast dishes like *idli*, *dosa*, *appam*, *idiyappam*, *puttu*, and *pathiri*.

Hindu cuisine

Many of Kerala's Hindus, except certain communities and ovolacto vegetarians, eat fish and chicken. Some communities, on the other hand, are famed for their vegetarian cuisine consisting of milk and dairy-based dishes, especially various varieties of sambar and rasam. In most Kerala households, a typical meal consists of rice, fish, and vegetables. Beef, contrary to the outlook of the remaining Indian society, also plays a prominent role in Kerala cuisine. The meat is featured in Hindu, Christian and Islamic communities of Kerala.

Sadhya

A typical sadya, where banana leaves are used as plates

Food offerings in rituals

Food is extremely important when it comes to rituals or festivals. Food offerings in ritual are important in Kerala and throughout South India. Food offerings are often related to the gods of religions. In India, there are numerous offerings for Hindu gods and there are many differences between food offerings in North and South India. Most offerings contain more than one type of food. There are many reasons why people use the practice of food offerings. Some are to express love, or negotiate or thank gods. It can also be used to "stress certain structural features of Hinduism". Of course, not every ritual's gods require food offerings. Most have a liking for certain foods. For example, butter is one of the preferred foods by the god Krishna. Also, wild orange and a sugarcane stalk are related to Ganapati.

There is a division of the Hindu pantheon into pure and impure deities which is stressed, but shaped by food offerings. Pure deities are offered vegetarian foods while impure deities are offered meat due to their craving for blood. A specific dish is offered to both pure and impure deities. That is a flour lamp which is made of sweetened rice-flour paste which is scooped out and packed with ghee. The flour lamp is only partially baked and then eaten. Another aspect of food offerings is the hierarchy that foods have. It may seem strange that there is a hierarchy for foods, but it is because there is a dual opposition between the pure and impure deities which is hierarchal. There are two gods which have this dual opposition. They are Vishnu and Siva. Ferro-Luzzi explains that Vishnu is viewed as kind while the offerings that are given to Siva are more frugal'. An offering to Siva might be likely to be plain rice with no salt or other toppings, while an offering to Vishnu may resemble a South Indian dish which can consist of rice with other side dishes. Specifically in South Indian offerings, they are offered in numbers. For example, the number three is important in Kerala offerings. There are the *trimadhura* which translates into 'the three sweets'.

Cooking as sacred ritual

The last decade has seen the rise of cooking as sacred ritual in South Kerala, almost exclusively by women. This practice, called 'Pongala' (derived from Tamil dish Pongal), seems to have been historically associated with the Attukal Temple in Trivandrum city which was begotten from Tamil tradition. According to the Guinness Book of Records, *Attukal Pongala* is the largest gathering of women in the world.

Often, the women take over most of the roads and lanes of Trivandrum city during the pongala day. In 2009, the estimated number of women who participated was 2.5 million.

The women wait until the Attukal temple ceremoniously distributes the fire, and set about their cooking when the fire reaches them, passed from hearth to hearth. They go home with the cooked offerings by late afternoon. While males are not allowed in the area, they help out by providing support to arriving and departing women by organising transportation, and distributing free beverages.

Cuisine of the Syrian Christians

Syrian Christians, or Mar Thoma Christians, of Kerala have their own cuisine. Particularly well-developed are the snacks and savouries of Syrian Christians such as "achappam' and "kuzhalappam". A favourite dish of Kerala Christians is "mappas", or chicken stew. For this dish, chicken, potatoes and onions are simmered gently in a creamy white sauce flavoured with black pepper, cinnamon, cloves, green chillies, lime juice, shallots and coconut milk. Lamb and duck can replace chicken in the stew recipe.

Other dishes include *piralen* (chicken stir-fries), *meat thoran* (dry curry with shredded coconut), sardine and duck curries, and meen molee (spicy stewed fish). This is eaten with another dish known as appam. *Appam*, *kallappam*, or *vellayappam* are rice flour pancakes which have soft, thick white spongy centres and crisp, lace-like edges. "Meen Mulakittathu" or "Meen vevichathu" (fish in fiery red chilly sauce) is another favourite item. "Pidi", a type of rice dumplings in thick gravy, is a famous Syrian Christian delicacy. "Pidi" is paired best with chicken curry.

In addition to chicken and fish, Syrian Christians along with a section of Hindus and all Muslims in Kerala eat red meat. "Irachi ularthiathu *is a beef dish cooked with spices.*

MODERN KERALA SOCIETY

Being the state with the highest literacy rate and education level in the country, the Kerala society has moved from its agricultural background. Although Kerala remains fairly liberal in its outlook and open to modern ideas,and technological changes, the State largely remains conservative on social issues.

Martial arts and sports

Kerala also has its own indigenous form of martial art - Kalarippayattu, derived from the words *kalari* ("place", "threshing floor", or "battlefield") and *payattu* ("exercise" or "practice"). Influenced by both Kerala's Brahminical past and Ayurvedic medicine, *kalaripayattu* is attributed by oral tradition to Parasurama. After some two centuries of suppression by British colonial authorities, it is now experiencing strong comeback among Keralites while also steadily gaining worldwide attention. Other popular ritual arts include *theyyam* and *poorakkali*— these originate from northern Malabar, which is the northernmost part of Kerala. Nevertheless, these have in modern times been largely supplanted by more popular sports such as cricket, kabaddi, soccer, badminton, and others. 'Kochi Tuskers Kerala' playing in the Indian Premier League (IPL) is from Kerala. Kerala is home of the football clubs Kerala Blasters, Gokulam Kerala FC, Viva Kerala and FC Kochin.

Calendar

Kerala also has an indigenous ancient solar calendar — the Malayalam calendar — which is used in various communities primarily for timing agricultural and religious activities.

Elephants in Kerala culture

The elephants are an integral part of the culture and daily life in Kerala. These Indian elephants are given a prestigious place in the state's culture. They are often christened names by which they're known across the entire state. Elephants in Kerala are often referred to as the 'sons of the *sahya'* and are indispensable for temple festivals. The elephant is the state animal of Kerala and is featured on the emblem of the Government of Kerala.

Sarpa Kavu (meaning *Sacred Grove of the Serpent*) is a typically small traditional grove of trees seen in the Kerala state of South India. These pristine groves usually have representations of several *Naga Devatas* (*serpent gods*), which were worshipped by the joint families or taravads. This was part of *Nagaradhana* (snake worship) which was prevalent among Keralites during past centuries. It had been practised by Thiyyas, Perumannans, Nairs, Arayas and many other tribal, non-tribal and coastal communities all over the Malabar Coast in South India. snake was considered as god and the people worshipped on them for getting blessings.

Caparisoned elephants during **Sree Poornathrayesa temple** *festival. The Elephants of Kerala are an integral part of the daily life in Kerala.*

Kerala has a large number of temples. The temples celebrate annual festivals which are not only unique to the region but sometimes have features that are unique to each temple. Each temple describes each interesting history behind its creation. In the Malabar, distinct art form called Theyyam attract tourists, and mini carnivals are also held along with temple festivals. Temple festivals are taken up with great pride by the residents and patrons of the temple and celebrated with much ado.

3

Government and Politics

GOVERNMENT OF KERALA

The Government of Kerala headquartered at Thiruvananthapuram is a democratically elected body that governs the Indian State of Kerala. The state government is headed by the Governor of Kerala as the nominal head of state, with a democratically elected Chief Minister as real head of the executive. The state government maintains its capital at Thiruvananthapuram (Trivandrum) and is seated at the Kerala Government Secretariat or the Hajur Kutcheri.

The Government of Kerala was formed on November 1, 1956 after merging of State of Travancore-Cochin with the Malabar district of the Madras state as part of States Reorganisation Act, 1956.

Government and administration

Governor

The Governor is appointed by the President for a term of five years. The executive and legislative powers lie with the Chief Minister and his council of ministers, who are appointed by the Governor. The Governors of the states and territories of India have similar powers and functions at the state level as that of the President of India at Union level. Only Indian citizens above 35 years of age are eligible for appointment. Governors discharge all constitutional functions such as the appointment of the Chief Minister, sending reports to the President about failure of constitutional machinery in a state, or with respect to issues relating to the assent to a bill passed by legislature, exercise or their own opinion.

P Sathasivam is the present governor. The Governor enjoys many different types of powers:

1. Executive powers related to administration, appointments and removals.
2. Legislative powers related to lawmaking and the state legislature.
3. Discretionary powers to be carried out according to the discretion of the Governor.

Legislature

The legislature comprises the governor and the legislative assembly, which is the highest political organ in state. The governor has the power to summon the assembly or to close the same. All members of the legislative assembly are directly elected, normally once in every five years by the eligible voters who are above 18 years of age. The current assembly consists of 140 elected members and one member nominated by the governor from the Anglo-Indian Community. The elected members select one of its own members as its chairman who is called the speaker. The speaker is assisted by the deputy speaker who is also elected by the members. The conduct of meeting in the house is the responsibility of the Speaker.

The main function of the assembly is to pass laws and rules. Every bill passed by the house has to be finally approved by the governor before it becomes applicable.

The normal term of the legislative assembly is five years from the date appointed for its first meeting. But while a proclamation of state of emergency is in operation, the said period will be extended by Parliament by Laws for a period not exceeding one year at a time.

Judiciary

High Court of Kerala in Kochi

The High Court of Kerala is the apex court for the state; it also hears cases from the Union Territory of Lakshadweep. It is a court of record and has all the powers of such a court including the authority to punish an individual for contempt of court. Like all other High Courts of India, this court also consists of a Chief Justice and other judges who are appointed by the President of India. At present, the sanctioned Judge strength of the High Court of Kerala is 27 Permanent Judges including the Chief Justice H.L. Dattu and two additional judges. Every judge including the Chief Justice is appointed by the President of India by Warrant under his hand and seal. Every permanent and additional judge will continue in office until the age of 62.

The High Court of Kerala is located in Kochi and there are courts in every district centres and some municipal centres.

Executive

Like in other Indian states, the Executive arm of the state is responsible for the day-to-day management of the state. It consists of the Governor, the Chief Minister and the Council of Ministers. The Chief Minister and the council of ministers also have been appointed by the governor. Governor summons prorogues and dissolves the legislature. He can close the legislative assembly on the recommendations by the Chief Minister. Judiciary has been separated from the executive in Kerala like other Indian states.

The Government Secretariat Complex in Thiruvananthapuram, which houses offices of ministers and secretaries

Chief Minister

The executive authority is headed by the Chief Minister of Kerala, who is the de facto head of state and is vested with most of the executive powers; the Legislative Assembly's majority party leader is appointed to this position by the Governor. The present Chief Minister is Pinarayi Vijayan, who took office on 25 May 2016. Generally, the winning party decides the chief minister. In many cases, the party focuses a chief ministerial candidate during the election.

Council of Ministers

The Council of Ministers, which answers to the Legislative Assembly, has its members appointed by the Governor; the appointments receive input from the Chief Minister. They are collectively responsible to the legislative assembly of the State. Generally, the winning party and its chief minister chooses the ministers list and submit the list for the Governor's approval.

Administrative divisions

Kerala State has been divided into 14 districts,27 revenue divisions,14 District Panchayats, 75 taluks, 152 CD blocks, 1453 revenue villages, 978 Gram panchayats, 6 corporations and 60 municipalities. The business of the state government is transacted through the various secretariat departments based on the rules of business. Each department consists of secretary to government, who is the official head of the department and such other under secretaries, junior secretaries, officers and staffs subordinate to him/her. The *Chief secretary* superintending control over the whole secretariat and staff attached to the ministers.

The department is further divided into sections, each of which is under the charge of a section officer. Apart from these sections, dealing with the subjects allotted to them, there are other offices sections, assigned with specific duties. When there is more than one secretary in a department, there shall be a clear separation of work.

Departments

- Finance Department
- Department of Registration (Kerala)
- Forests and Wildlife Department
- I&PRD Department
- NORKA Department
- PWD Department
- Tourism Department
- Revenue Department
- Civil Supplies Department
- Industries Department
- Education Department
- Agricultural Department
- Law Department
- Water Resources Department
- Health Services Department

- Animal Husbandry
- Fisheries & Ports
- Electronics & Information Technology
- Ayush
- Co-operation
- Home
- Health and Family Welfare
- Norka
- Housing
- Information & Public Relations
- Coastal Shipping and Inland Navigation
- Social Justice Department
- Local Self-Government Department
- Taxes
- Transport
- Vigilance
- Water Resources
- Western Ghats Cell
- Power
- Public Works Department
- SC/ST Development
- Science & Technology
- Planning & Economic Affairs

State insignias

The Kerala State Emblem is a derivative version of the Royal coat of arms of the Kingdom of Travancore. The state emblem symbolises two elephants guarding the Imperial Shanku in its Imperial crest. The Imperial Counch Crest or Shanku was the Imperial Insignia of Lord Sree Padmanabha (A form of Lord Vishnu)- the National Deity of Travancore. Shanku was considered as one of the common emblems of majority of Kerala feudal kingdoms. The Kingdom of Cochin and Zamorin's Malabar also had counch as state emblems. When the Kingdoms of Cochin and

Travancore merged in 1949, for a brief period, the crest carried a wheel or chakra in centre with *Shanku* on top of it. With accession of Malabar into Travancore-Cochin, the state of Kerala was formed in 1957. During this time, the royal coat of arms of the Travancore kingdom was modified by placing the "Lion Capital of Ashoka" on top of the Imperial conch. The Travancore Royal Family uses the erstwhile Royal Coat of Arms of Travancore today, whereas Sree Padmanabhaswamy Temple of Trivandrum uses only the Imperial Conch crest as its coat of arms.

Elections

Elections to the state assembly are held every five years. Elections are generally held for Parliament, State assembly and regional panchayats. Due to the large numbers of eligible voters, over 21 million, elections are usually held on several dates. Like all other Indian states, the minimum age of registration of a voter is 18 years.

Politics

Kerala has a unique position in India as one of the most politicised states. It has the nation's largest politically aware population, which actively participates in state politics.

Politics in Kerala is dominated by two political fronts: the CPI(M)led Left Democratic Front (LDF) and the Indian National Congress-led United Democratic Front (UDF) since late 1970s. These two coalitions have alternated in power since 1982. According to the 2016 Kerala Legislative Assembly election, the LDF has a majority in the state assembly (92/140).

The political alliance has strongly stabilised and, with rare exceptions, most of the coalition partners maintain loyalty to the alliance. As a result of this, power has alternated between these two fronts since 1979.

In terms of individual parties, the state has a strong leanings towards socialism and thus Communist parties have made strong inroads in Kerala. The Malabar region, particularly Kannur and Palakkad, are considered the heartland of the Communist parties. The Kollam and Alapuzha districts, where trade unions have a strong presence, are generally inclined to

Left parties, though several times the UDF has won. The CPI(M) led LDF did a clean sweep of 11-0 over UDF and NDA in Kollam district during 2016 Local body election. The largest Communist party is the CPIM and the second largest is the CPI.

The Indian National Congress, which leads the UDF coalition, has had a very strong presence in Kerala since pre-Independence days. The Congress party has great popularity in the Thrissur, Ernakulam, Kottayam, Pathanamthitta and Thiruvananthapuram regions, whereas it has a strong influence in some parts of Idukki regions.

The Bharathiya Janata Party (the Party that currently leads the Government of India) is also active in Kerala, but is not part of either coalition. It does not have any elected Parliament, but has one Legislative Assembly member and selected members in all the Corporations, several Municipal Councils and a large number of Local Panchayats. The party enjoys popularity in the districts of Thiruvananthapuram and Kasaragod. Other popular regional parties are

- The Kerala Congress, which has more than four denominations after breaking away from the original party. It has strong influence among settlement populations in hilly regions. The various Kerala Congress denominations are primarily patronized by the Syrian Christian community and Nair populations, mostly in Central Travancore areas like Kottayam, Idukki and Pathanamthitta. Today, most of Kerala Congress parties are with the UDF.
- The Indian Union Muslim League is a powerful pro-Muslim community-oriented party, which was started as the Muslim League prior to Independence, yet decided to transfer their allegiance to the Indian Union after Independence, when the original Muslim League went to Pakistan. The IUML-Kerala unit is the only Muslim League group to declare its allegiance and loyalty to India and hence become a state party in post-Independence India. The party has strongholds mostly in Muslim-dominated

districts like Kozhikode, Malappuram and Kasargod. They form the second largest party within the UDF.

- Socialist groups, consisting of several small fragmented parties like the NCP, SJD-S, JDS, and Congress-S, are mainly centre-left socialist parties having very limited influence in a few pocket areas. Most of the socialist groups are with the LDF, though in a few instances, some of them changed their loyalties to the UDF.
- Communist parties consist of various groups which have broken away from the CPIM. They are mostly centre-left parties, though a few are extreme-left. While a few centre-left parties like the RSP have joined with the LDF, those that broke away from the CPIM, like the CMP and JSS, led by erstwhile CPIM veterans who were expelled from CPIM, have joined with the UDF.
- The Bharath Dharma Jana Sena or BDJS is a new political party formed in 2015 led by Thushar Vellapally. The party's primary vote base is among Ezhava and thiyya community. It is politically and ideologically aligned towards the BJP and is a part of National Democratic Alliance.

GOVERNMENT AND ADMINISTRATION

The Kerala High Court complex in Kochi.

The Kerala Secretariat in Thiruvananthapuram – seat of executive administration of Kerala, and formerly of the legislative assembly

The Kerala Legislative AssemblyBuilding in Thiruvananthapuram

Kerala hosts two major political alliances: the United Democratic Front (UDF), led by the Indian National Congress; and the Left Democratic Front (LDF), led by the Communist Party of India (Marxist) (CPI(M)). As of 2016, the LDF is the ruling coalition; Pinarayi Vijayan of the Communist Party of India (Marxist) is the Chief Minister, while Ramesh Chennithala of the UDF is the Leader of Opposition. Strikes, protests and marches are ubiquitous in Kerala because of the comparatively strong presence of labour unions. According to the Constitution of India, Kerala has a parliamentary system of representative democracy; universal suffrage is granted to residents. The government is organised into the three branches:

1. Legislature: The unicameral legislature, the Kerala Legislative Assembly popularly known as Niyamasabha, comprises elected members and special office bearers; the Speaker and Deputy Speaker elected by the members from among themselves. Assembly meetings are presided over by the Speaker and in the Speaker's absence, by the Deputy Speaker. The state has 140 assembly constituencies. The state elects 20 and 9 members for representation in the Lok Sabha and the Rajya Sabha respectively.
2. Executive: The Governor of Kerala is the constitutional head of state, and is appointed by the President of India. P Sathasivam is the Governor of Kerala. The executive authority is headed by the Chief Minister of Kerala, who is the head of government and is vested with extensive executive powers; the head of the majority party in the Legislative Assembly is appointed to the post by the Governor. The Council of Ministers has its members appointed by the Governor, taking the advice of the Chief Minister. The executive administration is based in Thiruvananthapuram at State Secretariat complex. Each district has a district administrator appointed by government called District collector for executive administration. Auxiliary authorities known as *panchayats*, for which local body elections are regularly held, govern local affairs.
3. Judiciary: The judiciary consists of the Kerala High Court and a system of lower courts. The High Court, located in Kochi, has a Chief Justice along with 23 permanent and seven additional *pro tempore* justices as of 2012. The high court also hears cases from the Union Territory of Lakshadweep.

The local government bodies; Panchayat, Municipalities and Corporations have existed in Kerala since 1959, however, the major initiative to decentralise the governance was started in 1993, conforming to the constitutional amendments of central government in this direction.With the enactment of Kerala Panchayati Raj Act and Kerala Municipality Act in 1994, the state implemented reforms in local self-governance. The Kerala Panchayati Raj Act envisages a 3-tier system of local government with Gram panchayat, Block panchayat and District Panchayat forming a hierarchy. The acts ensure a clear demarcation of power among these institutions. However, the Kerala Municipality Act envisages a single-tier system for urban areas, with the institution of municipality designed to par with the Gram panchayat of the former system. Substantial administrative, legal and financial powers are delegated to these bodies to ensure efficient decentralisation. As per the present norms, the state government devolves about 40 per cent of the state plan outlay to the local government.

KERALA LEGISLATIVE ASSEMBLY

The Kerala Legislative Assembly, popularly known as the Niyamasabha (literally *Hall of laws*), is the law making body of Kerala, one of the 29 States in India. The Assembly is formed by 140 elected representatives and one nominated member from the Anglo-Indian community. Each elected member represents one of the 140 constituencies within the borders of Kerala and is referred to as Member of the Legislative Assembly (MLA).

History

The evolution of Kerala Legislative Assembly begins with the formation of a Legislative Council in the princely state of Travancore in 1888. This was the first Native Legislature in the Indian subcontinent, outside British India. The Legislative Council of Travancore had undergone many changes by years. In the meantime, people's participation in the Assembly was widely sought. All those efforts led to the formation of one more representative body, namely the Sri Moolam Popular Assembly of Travancore. This Assembly of the representatives of the landholders and merchants, aimed at giving the people an opportunity of bringing to the notice of Government their requirements, wishes or grievances on the one hand, and on the other, to make the policy and measures of Government better known to the people so that all possible grounds of misconception may be removed.

That was on 1 October 1904. Though the popular assembly contained representatives of tax-payers, it finally became a people's representatives body. Political awareness and people agitations were aggressive and the authorities were forced to include peoples representatives into the popular assembly. On 1 May 1905, a regulation was issued to grant to the people the privilege of electing members to the Assembly. Of the 100 members, 77 were to be elected and 23 nominated, for a tenure of 1 year. The right to vote was given to persons who paid on their account an annual land revenue of not less than Rs. 50 or whose net income was not less than Rs. 2000 and to graduates of a recognised University, with not less than 10 years standing and having their residence in the taluk. The membership of the popular assembly increased year by year and finally in 1921 elected representatives gained the majority. By that time the house had 50 members of which 28 were elected and the rest nominated.

The princely state of Cochin also formed a *Legislative Council* (1925), with 30 elected and 15 nominated representatives. Malabar District of Madras Province under the British rule, had representatives in Madras Legislative Assembly from the 1920s.

After India's independence responsible governments were formed in Travancore and Cochin. In 1949 the merger of Travancore and Cochin as Travancore-Cochin, formed the first Legislative Assembly, the Travancore-Cochin Legislative Assembly composed of 178 members of the Legislative bodies of Travancore and Cochin. The Malabar region had representatives in the Madras Legislative Assembly.

Assembly after the formation of Kerala State

In 1956, the State of Kerala was formed on linguistic basis, merging Travancore, Cochin and Malabar regions. The first assembly election in Kerala state was held in February-March 1957. The first *Kerala Legislative Assembly* was formed on 5 April 1957. The Assembly had 127 members including a nominated member.

Subsequently, after formation of Malappuram and Kasargod districts, the number of seats went up to 140. The current delimitation committee of 2010 reaffirmed the total number of seats at 140.

Current assembly

The current Legislative Assembly is the 14th Assembly since the formation of Kerala. The Speaker of the Assembly is P. Sreeramakrishnan.

The leader of the Assembly is Pinarayi Vijayan from CPI(M) and the Leader of the Opposition is Ramesh Chennithala from the INC. At the same time, the deputy leader of opposition is M. K. Muneer of IUML.

Niyamasabha Complex

The State Assembly is known as Niyama Sabha and is housed in New Legislature Complex. This 5 storied complex is one of the largest complexes in India. The Central Hall is described as most elegant and majestic hall with ornamental Teakwood-Rosewood panelling. The older Assembly was located within State Secretariat complex which was reconverted into Legislature museum, after commissioning new complex in 1998 May 22 (K. R. Narayanan)

Political parties or coalitions

No:	Front/Alliance	Seats
1	Left Democratic Front	91
2	United Democratic Front	46
3	National Democratic Alliance	1
4	Independent	1
5	Vacant	1

Members

The entrance to Kerala Legislature with statute of Mahatma Gandhi

The Illuminated Niyamasabha Complex at night

Kerala State Legislative Assembly or the Niyamasabha at night

S. N:	Constituency	Winner	Party
1	Manjeshwar	Vacant	
2	Kasaragod	N. A. Nellikkunnu	IUML
3	Udma	K. Kunhiraman	CPI(M)
4	Kanhangad	E. Chandrasekharan	CPI
5	Trikarpur	M. Rajagopalan	CPI(M)
6	Payyanur	C. Krishnan	CPI(M)
7	Kalliasseri	T. V. Rajesh	CPI(M)
8	Taliparamba	James Mathew	CPI(M)
9	Irikkur	K. C. Joseph	INC
10	Azhikode	K.M. Shaji	IUML
11	Kannur	Kadannappalli Ramachandran	Cong(S)
12	Dharmadom	Pinarayi Vijayan	CPI(M)
13	Thalassery	A. N. Shamseer	CPI(M)
14	Kuthuparamba	K. K. Shailaja	CPI(M)
15	Mattannur	E. P. Jayarajan	CPI(M)
16	Peravoor	Sunny Joseph	INC
17	Mananthavady	O. R. Kelu	CPI(M)
18	Sulthanbathery	I. C. Balakrishnan	INC
19	Kalpetta	C. K. Saseendran	CPI(M)
20	Vatakara	C. K. Nanu	JD(S)
21	Kuttiady	Parakkal Abdulla	IUML
22	Nadapuram	E. K. Vijayan	CPI
23	Koyilandy	K. Dasan	CPI(M)
24	Perambra	T. P. Ramakrishnan	CPI(M)
25	Balusseri	Purushan Kadalundy	CPI(M)
26	Elathur	A. K. Saseendran	NCP

27	Kozhikode North	A. Pradeepkumar	CPI(M)
28	Kozhikode South	M. K. Muneer	IUML
29	Beypore	V. K. C. Mammed Koya	CPI(M)
30	Kunnamangalam	P. T. A. Rahim	LDF Independent
31	Koduvally	Karat Razak	LDF Independent
32	Thiruvambady	George M. Thomas	CPI(M)
33	Kondotty	T. V. Ibrahim	IUML
34	Ernad	P. K. Basheer	IUML
35	Nilambur	P. V. Anvar	LDF Independent
36	Wandoor	A.P. Anil Kumar	INC
37	Manjeri	M. Ummer	IUML
38	Perinthalmanna	Manjalamkuzhi Ali	IUML
39	Mankada	T. A. Ahmed Kabir	IUML
40	Malappuram	P. Ubaidulla	IUML
41	Vengara	K. N. A. Khader	IUML
42	Vallikunnu	P. Abdul Hameed	IUML
43	Tirurangadi	P. K. Abdu Rabb	IUML
44	Tanur	V. Abdurahiman	LDF Independent
45	Tirur	C. Mammutty	IUML
46	Kottakkal	K. K. Abid Hussain Thangal	IUML
47	Thavanur	K.T. Jaleel	LDF Independent
48	Ponnani	P. Sreeramakrishnan	CPI(M)
49	Thrithala	V. T. Balram	INC
50	Pattambi	Muhammed Muhsin	CPI
51	Shornur	P. K. Sasi	CPI(M)
52	Ottappalam	P. Unni	CPI(M)
53	Kongad	K. V. Vijayadas	CPI(M)
54	Mannarkkad	N. Samsudheen	IUML
55	Malampuzha	V. S. Achuthanandan	CPI(M)
56	Palakkad	Shafi Parambil	INC
57	Tarur	A. K. Balan	CPI(M)
58	Chittur	K. Krishnankutty	JD(S)
59	Nemmara	K. Babu	CPI(M)
60	Alathur	K. D. Prasenan	CPI(M)
61	Chelakkara	U. R. Pradeep	CPI(M)
62	Kunnamkulam	A. C. Moideen	CPI(M)
63	Guruvayoor	K. V. Abdul Khader	CPI(M)
64	Manalur	Murali Perunelli	CPI(M)
65	Wadakkanchery	Anil Akkara	INC

66	Ollur	K. Rajan	CPI
67	Thrissur	V. S. Sunil Kumar	CPI
68	Nattika	Geetha Gopi	CPI
69	Kaipamangalam	E. T. Tyson	CPI
70	Irinjalakuda	K. U. Arunan	CPI(M)
71	Puthukkad	C. Raveendranath	CPI(M)
72	Chalakudy	B. D. Devassy	CPI(M)
73	Kodungallur	V. R. Sunil Kumar	CPI
74	Perumbavoor	Eldhose Kunnappilly	INC
75	Angamaly	Roji M. John	INC
76	Aluva	Anwar Sadath	INC
77	Kalamassery	V. K. Ebrahimkunju	IUML
78	Paravur	V. D. Satheesan	INC
79	Vypeen	S. Sharma	CPI(M)
80	Kochi	K. J. Maxi	CPI(M)
81	Thripunithura	M. Swaraj	CPI(M)
82	Ernakulam	Hibi Eden	INC
83	Thrikkakara	P. T. Thomas	INC
84	Kunnathunad (SC)	V.P. Sajeendran	INC
85	Piravom	Anoop Jacob	KC (Jacob)
86	Muvattupuzha	Eldo Abraham	CPI
87	Kothamangalam	Antony John	CPI(M)
88	Devikulam	S. Rajendran	CPI(M)
89	Udumbanchola	M. M. Mani	CPI(M)
90	Thodupuzha	P. J. Joseph	KC(M)
91	Idukki	Roshy Augustine	KC(M)
92	Peerumade	E. S. Bijimol	CPI
93	Pala	K. M. Mani	KC(M)
94	Kaduthuruthy	Monce Joseph	KC(M)
95	Vaikom	C. K. Asha	CPI
96	Ettumanoor	K. Suresh Kurup	CPI(M)
97	Kottayam	Thiruvanchoor Radhakrishnan	INC
98	Puthuppally	Oommen Chandy	INC
99	Changanassery	C. F. Thomas	KC(M)
100	Kanjirappally	N. Jayaraj	KC(M)
101	Poonjar	P. C. George	INDEPENDENT
102	Aroor	A. M. Ariff	CPI(M)
103	Cherthala	P. Thilothaman	CPI
104	Alappuzha	T. M. Thomas Isaac	CPI(M)
105	Ambalappuzha	G. Sudhakaran	CPI(M)

106	Kuttanad	Thomas Chandy	NCP
107	Haripad	Ramesh Chennithala	INC
108	Kayamkulam	Prathiba Hari	CPI(M)
109	Mavelikkara	R. Rajesh	CPI(M)
110	Chengannur	Saji Cherian	CPI(M)
111	Thiruvalla	Mathew T. Thomas	JD(S)
112	Ranni	Raju Abraham	CPI(M)
113	Aranmula	Veena George	CPI(M)
114	Konni	Adoor Prakash	INC
115	Adoor	Chittayam Gopakumar	CPI
116	Karunagapally	R. Ramachandran	CPI
117	Chavara	Vijayan Pillai	CMP
118	Kunnathur	Kovoor Kunjumon	RSP Independent
119	Kottarakkara	P. Aisha Potty	CPI(M)
120	Pathanapuram	K. B. Ganesh Kumar	KC(B)
121	Punalur	K. Raju	CPI
122	Chadayamangalam	Mullakara Ratnakaran	CPI
123	Kundara	J. Mercykutty Amma	CPI(M)
124	Kollam	M. Mukesh	CPI(M)
125	Eravipuram	M. Noushad	CPI(M)
126	Chathannoor	G.S. Jayalal	CPI
127	Varkala	V. Joy	CPI(M)
128	Attingal	B. Satyan	CPI(M)
129	Chirayinkeezhu	V. Sasi	CPI
130	Nedumangad	C. Divakaran	CPI
131	Vamanapuram	D. K. Murali	CPI(M)
132	Kazhakoottam	Kadakampally Surendran	CPI(M)
133	Vattiyoorkavu	K. Muraleedharan	INC
134	Thiruvananthapuram	V. S. Sivakumar	INC
135	Nemam	O. Rajagopal	BJP
136	Aruvikkara	K. S. Sabarinathan	INC
137	Parassala	C. K. Hareendran	CPI(M)
138	Kattakkada	I. B. Sathish	CPI(M)
139	Kovalam	M. Vincent	INC
140	Neyyattinkara	K. A. Ansalan	CPI(M)

Composition

The Assembly consists of 140 Members known as Members of Legislative Assembly- MLA representing each constituency.

The qualifications needed to become an MLA are almost similar to the eligibility criteria for an MP. Besides being a citizen of India, the individual should not be less than 25 years of age. On a more fundamental note, a person, who is not a voter from any constituency of the state, is not eligible to become an MLA.

It's to be noted that an MLA is elected by the people of a particular constituency and he/she represents those electorates in the Legislative Assembly. MLAs enjoy the same position in the state as MPs on a national level.

Responsibilities of Legislators

The principal responsibility of an MLA is to represent the people's grievances and aspirations and take them up with the state government. An MLA has the power to utilise several legislative tools including 'calling attention motion' to raise issues concerning his/her constituency. It's also expected of the MLA to raise the issues with the relevant government agency and minister. As a legislator, his cardinal role will be to make optimum use of the Local Area Development (LAD) fund in a bid to develop his constituency.

Appointment of Speaker

The Speaker is the primary official of the Assembly. The Assembly elects the Speaker from among its own members. While the Speaker still represents his constituency, he remains an impartial chair of the Assembly and refrains from debating.

When a new assembly is formed, the political party/alliance which is invited by the Governor to form a government, nominates one among them as Pro-term Speaker. The Pro-Term speaker swears in front of Governor and opens the new assembly's first session.

He oversees swearing-in ceremony of all legislators at the assembly hall and then becomes the returning officer for the Speaker Election.

The Leader of the House, Chief Minister presents a motion for speaker election and nominates one among his party/alliance for Speaker position.

The Leader of Opposition supports the motion and nominates one among them as speaker position. The Pro-term speaker then asks whether anyone else wish to contest for speaker post. If any application received, it shall also be enlisted for election.

Based on motion, the pro-term speaker will order for an election and Legislative secretary will arrange an election at the floor of the assembly. The election will be closed affair with each member casting a secret vote on a ballot paper. The results will be counted by Legislative Secretary in front of representatives from both Ruling and Opposition parties.

Accordingly, the pro-term speaker announces the new speaker and both leaders of assembly escort the new speaker to Speaker Dias to take charge of the post.

A similar election is conducted to appoint Deputy Speaker who shall take the office in absence of the speaker.

Officials

The speaker is assisted by Legislative Secretariat. The head of Secretariat is Legislative Secretary. The Legislative secretary is the Executive chief of the Assembly and reports only to Speaker and house directly.

The Legislative secretary is supported by 2 Additional Secretaries, Joint Secretaries and Assistant Secretaries. There are under-secretaries for each committee topic and officers in charge.

The Chief Curator manages the entire house activities including housekeeping, maintenance and safety measures. The Chief Editor manages an editorial team to draft questions raised by public and legislators as well as manages answers notes, legislative records, executive orders and archival matters. The Chief Librarian manages the Central Library and Legislative Research cell of Niyamasabha.

Security

From days of Monarchy Kerala Police were not allowed inside Niyamasabha as a matter of enforcing legislative independence. The Niyamasabha has its own security force called Watch and

Ward, distinguished by its white uniforms who reports to Assembly Privileges committee and Speaker directly. Its headed by Chief Warden who is in the rank of Superintendent of Police.

The Watch and ward control the security of entire Assembly area as well as nearby Legislative Hostel.

Committees

Statutory Committee

The Niyamasabha consists of following committees which are statutory in nature and cannot be disbanded, though the members do change.

1. Business Advisory Committee (BAC): The BAC is the primary committee to decide the agendas to be listed in each session of the assembly. As a convention, the opposition leader will be the head of the committee with leaders of each parliamentary party subjected to a maximum of 8 members. Speaker of the house is a permanent invitee to this committee.
2. Committee on Environment
3. Committee on Estimates
4. Committee on Government Assurances
5. Committee on Local Fund Accounts
6. Committee on Official Language
7. Committee on Papers Laid on the Table
8. Committee on Petitions
9. Committee on Private Members' Bills and Resolutions
10. Committee on Privileges and Ethics
11. Committee on Public Accounts
12. Committee on Public Undertakings
13. Committee on Subordinate Legislation
14. Committee on the Welfare of Backward Class Communities
15. Committee on the Welfare of Fishermen and Allied Workers
16. Committee on the Welfare of Non-resident Keralites

17. Committee on the Welfare of Scheduled Castes and Scheduled Tribes
18. Committee on the Welfare of Senior Citizens
19. Committee on the Welfare of Women, Children and Physically Handicapped
20. Committee on the Welfare of Youth and Youth Affairs
21. House Committee
22. Library Advisory Committee
23. Rules Committee

Subject Committee

Apart from the statutory committee, the assembly has a subject committee for each Department of Government. Though they are not statutory in nature, its established by the house on regular basis to monitor and control executive decisions of each department when a specific bill intended to make into a legislation comes before assembly. Normally when a bill is presented and amendments or disputes arise, the bills are sent to a subject committee specifically formed such departmental activity.

As per Kerala Legislature Rules, the following committees are regularly established in the house.

1. Subject Committee - I:- Departments of Agriculture, Animal Husbandry and Fisheries
2. Subject Committee - II:- Land Revenue, Land usage, wetland protection, Endowments and Devaswom
3. Subject Committee - III:- Water Resources, Irrigation projects and Dam safety
4. Subject Committee - IV:- Industry and Minerals
5. Subject Committee - V:- Public Works, Transport & Communications
6. Subject Committee - VI:- Education
7. Subject Committee - VII:- Power, Labour and Labour Welfare
8. Subject Committee - VIII:- Economic Affairs

9. Subject Committee - IX:- Local Administration, Rural Development and Housing
10. Subject Committee - X:- Forest, Environment and Tourism
11. Subject Committee - XI:- Food, Civil Supplies and Co-operation
12. Subject Committee - XII:- Health and Family Welfare
13. Subject Committee - XIII:- Social Service
14. Subject Committee - XIV:- Home and Security Affairs

Ad-Hoc Committee

Time-to-time, the assembly can form an ad-hoc committee for business as laid by a motion passed by the house.

CHIEF MINISTERS OF KERALA

The Chief Minister of Kerala is the chief executive of the south Indian state of Kerala. In accordance with the Constitution of India, the governor is a state's *de jure* head, but *de facto* executive authority rests with the chief minister. Following elections to the Kerala Legislative Assembly, the state's governor usually invites the party (or coalition) with a majority of seats to form the government. The governor appoints the chief minister, whose council of ministers are collectively responsible to the assembly. Given that he has the confidence of the assembly, the chief minister's term is for five years and is subject to no term limits.

The origins of Kerala lie in the princely states of Travancore and Cochin. Following India's independence from the British Raj in 1947, these states' monarchs instituted a measure of representative government, headed by a Prime Minister and his Council of Ministers. On 1 July 1949 Travancore and Cochin were merged to form Travancore-Cochin state. On 1 November 1956, the States Reorganisation Act redrew India's map along linguistic lines, and the present-day state of Kerala was born, consisting solely of Malayalam-speaking districts. Since then, 12 people have served as the Chief Minister of Kerala. The first was E. M. S. Namboodiripad of the Communist Party of India, whose tenure was cut short by the imposition of President's rule. Kerala has come under President's rule for four years over seven terms, the last of them in 1982. Since then the office has alternated between leaders of the Indian National Congress and of the Communist Party of India (Marxist). The latter party's Pinarayi Vijayan is the incumbent chief minister; his Left Democratic Front government has been in office since 25 May 2016.

ELECTIONS IN KERALA

Elections in Kerala are regularly held to fill government officials at all levels of government in both Kerala and India as a whole. These range from national elections to regional local body or *panchayat* elections. The Assembly of Kerala creates laws regarding the conduct of local body elections unilaterally while any changes by the state legislature to the conduct of state level elections need to be approved by the Parliament of India. In addition, the state legislature may be dismissed by the Parliament according to Article 356 of the Indian Constitution and President's rule may be imposed.

Local Self Government institutions

Panchayat Elections is a term widely used in Kerala, India, for the polls that are held to select the *Local Self-government Representatives*. There are three branches of local self-government institutions in Kerala. They are *Grama Panchayat* which can be translated as Village Government, *Block Panchayat* and *District Panchayat*. A Grama Panchayat is almost an equivalent to City administration and District Panchayat to a County. There are two more wings namely Municipality which is another form of Block Panchayat that exists only in major towns and *Corporations* that come only in six major cities.

The State has 978 *Grama Panchayats*, 152 *Block Panchayats*, 14 *District Panchayats*, 60 *Municipalities* and 6 *Corporations*. Consequent to the 73rd Amendment to the Constitution of India, the local self-government institutions (LSGIs) are to function as the third tier of government. In Kerala, LSGIs have been meaningfully empowered through massive transfer of resources as well as administrative powers. Coupled with a grassroots level approach of participatory planning whereby the developmental programmes are identified and implemented through *Grama Sabhas* (Ward councils), the LSGIs have emerged as effective agencies for the implementation of developmental programmes.State Election Commission, Kerala came into existence on 3 December 1993 as envisaged in Article 243(k) of the Constitution of India. The superintendence, direction and control of preparation of voters list and conduct of election to the local self-government Institution vest with the Commission.

Dates

The last *Election to the Local Self-government Institutions in Kerala* (*Panchayat Elections*) was held in October 2015. Elections to the local bodies were held in two stages.The results for all were October.

The latest Assembly elections were held on May 16, 2016.

POLITICS OF KERALA

Political activity in the Indian State of Kerala takes place in a multi-party framework, within the overall context of the National Politics of India. The state holds an invariable position of having the largest politically aware and active population in the Country. The state Legislatureis unicameral and has a membership of 141, where 140 are elected and one is nominated from the Anglo-Indian community. It has 20 seats in the Lok Sabha and 9 seats in the Rajya Sabha. Elections are also held to choose representatives to the civic bodies at various levels within the State, and the state has consistently come out with a voter turnout of 70% or above in almost all elections which have ever been held.

The background

Politics in Kerala is dominated by two coalition fronts: the Communist Party of India(Marxist)-led Left Democratic Front (LDF) and the Indian National Congress-led United Democratic Front (UDF) since late 1970s. These two coalitions have been alternatively voted to power since 1982. Most of the major political parties in Kerala, except for Bharatiya Janata Party(BJP), belong to one or the other of these two alliances and have in the past shifting allegiances a number of times. In Kerala, it is difficult for a single party to contest and win even a single seat, because the voter perception is towards voting for a front. The BJP has been able to register its presence with one seat in Nemom in the assembly in spite of the fact that it is the third largest party in Kerala after Congress and CPM. According to 2016 Kerala Legislative Assembly election results, the LDF has a majority in the State Assembly(91/140). The political alliances have stabilized strongly in such a manner that, with rare exceptions, most of the coalition partners stick their loyalty to the respective alliances. As a result of this, ever since 1979, the power has been clearly alternating between the two fronts without any exceptions. However, till then the political scenario in Kerala was characterized by continually shifting alliances, party mergers and splits, factionalism within the coalitions and within political parties, and the formation of a numerous splinter groups. The political scenario has changed in Kerala and currently majority of news events are happening with respect to actions taken by political parties in Kerala.

Leftist inclination

The social thought and behavior of the State in general has a strong inclination towards Leftism and thus the Communist parties have made strong inroads in Kerala. The Malabar region, particularly Kannur and Palakkad are considered to heartland of Communist parties. The Kollam and Alapuzha districts, where trade unions have very strong presence, are generally inclined towards the Left parties; though the UDF have won elections from the constituencies of these districts several times. The largest Communist party in terms of membership is CPI (M) and the second is CPI. Kerala was the first Indian state where the communists were voted to power. Indian National Congress also has a very strong presence in Kerala. The party has strong bases in Ernakulam and Kottayam regions.

Regional parties

Chief Minister Pinarayi Vijayan is a communist leader

- Indian Union Muslim League, is a powerful pro-Muslim community oriented party, which was started as Muslim League prior to partition of India, yet decided to retain their allegiance to India after partition, when the original Muslim League went to Pakistan. The IUML-Kerala unit is the only Muslim League unit, which declared its allegiance and loyalty to India, and hence became a state party, in post-independent India. The party has strongholds mostly in Muslim dominated districts like Malappuram. and they form the second largest party within UDF. Mass population of Muslims in Malappuram supports the Indian Union Muslim League in most of the elections.
- Kerala Congress, which has more than 4 denominations, after breaking away from original party, has strong influence among settlement populations in hilly regions. The various Kerala Congress denominations are primarily

patronized by Syrian Christian community mostly in Central Travancore areas like Kottayam, Idukki, Pathanamthitta and Muvattupuzha. Today, most of Kerala Congress parties are with UDF.

- Socialist groups, consisting of several small fragmented parties like NCP, SJD-S, JDS, Congress-S, are mainly pro-center left socialist parties having very limited influences in few pocket areas. Most of the socialist groups are with LDF, though at few instances, some of them changed their loyalties to UDF.
- Communist parties, consists of various communist parties, which have broken away from CPIM which mostly are Center left parties and few are extreme left. While a few centre left parties like RSP have joined with LDF, those broken away from CPIM, like CMP, JSS etc., led by erstwhile CPIM veterans who were expelled from CPIM have joined with UDF.
- The All India Forward Bloc, which had associated with the LDF broken away from them and joined in the UDF in 2017. Now the AIFB is an active partner of UDF.
- Kerala Dalit Federation
- Indian Gandhiyan Party WE STAND FOR UPGRADING OUR NATION One India, #1 India Transform India being a developing country to No.1 Developed Country among the 193 UN approved Countries Educate every Indian to be self reliant & self financed, bring up a self reliant Indian Economy Empower Young Generation through Entrepreneurship, and bring Indian GDP more than 50% of World Economy. Every Indian will be contributing an Indian brand to the world Economy Increase the value of Indian rupee. Protect the Indian Ecosystem, Forests and Wild Life Focus on Research & Development in Science, Technology and International Affairs Ensure a better Standard of Living to Rural India Proactive Security to Indian Population, against Natural Disaster, Terrorism, Poverty, Unemployment or any kind of uncertainties.

Coalition politics

The first coalition government in Kerala was formed in 1960 and was headed by Pattom A. Thanu Pillai. The alliance comprised PSP, Congress and Muslim League. Pillai resigned in February 1962 after being appointed as Punjab governor and R. Sankar of Congress became Chief Minister. He also resigned in September 1964 after a no-confidence motion was passed in the Assembly. After the 1965 election, no party was able to form a government due to the fractured nature of results. The assembly was dissolved and the state was under Presidents Rule. In the 1967 election, a seven-party alliance named Saptakakshi Munnani won the election. This coalition also did not last long. In the 1970 election, CPI and Congress led Aikya Munanni emerged victorious and continued in power till 1979.

In 1980s, two main political coalitions were formed: the leftist Left Democratic Front, led by the Communist Party of India (Marxist) and the Centrist United Democratic Front, led by the Indian National Congress. Since the early 1980s these two coalitions have alternated in government with neither Front able to gain re-election for a second term. Clashes between supporters of the two coalitions have occurred periodically. Both the INC and the CPI(M) have accused the other of corruption, promoting or condoning political violence, and "the general breakdown of law and order" during their periods in government.

The Student Federation of India (SFI) is the student arm of the CPI(M), while the Kerala Student Union (KSU) is a pioneer of the students' movement of the INC. The two major parties and their student wings have a long history of enmity in Kerala.

Bandhs and Harthals

Direct action and political violence has become the characteristics of Kerala society in India. The state treasury of Kerala has suffered losses of thousands of millions of rupees, thanks to the state staging over 100 hartals annually in recent times. A record total of 223 harthals were observed in 2006, resulting in a revenue loss of over 2000 crore. There were around 363 of "Hartals", called by different political parties, between 2005 and 2012. Hartals are called for various reasons, political, economic and social. According to the Organisor, Kerala has the highest level of loss of manhours due to industrial unrest and the state has organized the highest number of strikes and harthals in the country.

The epicenter of violence

Kannur is the most violent district in Kerala. During the last 45 years, about 180 people were killed because of political violence in Kannur district of Kerala.

Kannur is historically linked with rebellion because Guerrilla King Pazhassi Raja fought against the British in this region. Kannur is the homeland of communist veterans like A K Gopalan, E K Nayanar and Azhikodan Raghavan. Most of the victims in political are from the toddy tapper community, which a branch of the Thiyya caste.

RSS - CPI (M) rows

Most often the fight in Kerala is between CPIM and RSS. A few years ago, in retaliation to what happened in Kannur, RSS workers attacked the CPI-M's national headquarters in Delhi, the CPI-M state secretary in Karnataka, Visakhapatnam and Madurai on the same day.

Social cohesion

That being said, Kerala has been the first state in India to openly accommodate the Transgender community. From transgender pageants to sporting events Kerala strives to provide equal opportunities to the repressed. It was also the first state to pass and implement an exclusive policy for the social and economic growth of the transgender community, employed 23 in the recently operational Kochi Metro and opened a school where dropouts and aspirants could pursue their education barring gender stereotypes. High profile politicians and actors such as Shashi Tharoor, Pinarayi Vijayan, Aju Varghese and Vineeth Srinivasan to name a few, had expressed their disapproval publicly of the BJP enforced beef ban and the subsequent attacks in other states pertaining to the same issue.

Kerala has been widely hailed as a state where people from every community happily coexists with Christian nuns dancing the "thiruvathira" which was traditionally a danceform prevalent amongst the upper-caste Hindu Nair community. The situation has changed a lot, the society is now much more tolerant to change, especially in the cities.

Kiss of Love protest

Kiss of Love protest is a non-violent protest against moral policing which started in Kerala, India, and later spread to other parts of India. The movement began when a Facebook page called 'Kiss of love' called forth the youth across Kerala to participate in a protest against moral policing on November 2, 2014, at Marine Drive, Cochin. The movement received widespread support with more than 154,404 'Likes' for the Facebook page. After the initial protest in Kochi, similar protests were organised in other major cities of the country. It received opposition from various religious and political groups like Bharatiya Janata Yuva Morcha, SDPI, Vishva Hindu Parishad, Shiv Sena, Bajrang Dal, Hindu Sena and Ernakulam wing of Kerala Students Union. On specific occasions but not exclusively, both the Supreme Court of India and Delhi High Court have made it clear that kissing in public is not an obscene act and no criminal proceedings can be initiated, for kissing in public, through landmark judgments.

4

Language and Literature

Kerala is one first Indian state with a literacy level of 100%. Both Malayalam and English are widely taught Language in the state. Malayalam is, however, the regional and official Language of the state. Malayalam is also one of the official Language of India. It is essentially a Dravidian Language but historical events have influenced the growth and vocabulary of Malayalam.

The original Dravidian settlers commonly used Tamil as their Language. Tamil was the court Language in the Chera regime too. Around the 10th century, Malayalam started to develop its own distinctive character. Due to the common grammar and vocabulary, many scholars feel Malayalam is like an offspring of Tamil; however Malayalam has a rich modern literature and an independent written script (Kolezhethu). With the settling of the Aryans, Sanskrit put the growth of Malayalam on a bane. The Brahmin Namboodiris exclusively used Sanskrit but this incidence, instead of threatening the existence of Malayalam enriched it instead. The local Language absorbed the words from Sanskrit and used them with a Malayali addition or alteration. Thus evolved the Mani Pravlam or Malayalam heavily spiked with usage of Sanskrit words.

Current day Malayalam has about 53 letters of which 20 are long/short vowels and the rest are consonants. Since 1981, the script was modified to adapt Malayalam to the use of keyboard and hence there are currently only 90 letters for a typeset.

Variations in the Language can be seen across the length and breadth of the state depending on social structure, geography and community. The Syriac Christians' vocabulary is influenced by English, Syriac, Latin and Portuguese while the Muslim population talks Malayali with additions from Urdu, Arabic. Sanskrit influences the Brahmin lingo the most. Pali is another Language that has influenced the native tongue.

The other major Language spoken in the state and hence another big influence on Malayalam is English. The European association and the British rule have lent this characteristic to the state. The inhabitants of Pallakad and border regions speak Tamil and those of Northern Kerala are influenced by the Konkan and Marathi Language. The Language has 5 main dialects

Since the 19th century, Malayalam literature has undergone tremendous growth. Original novels, poetry, play, prose and lyrics have truly flourished. T. M. Appu Netunnati's Kundalata (1887) and Chantu Menon's Indulekha (1889) were among the first novels in the Language. Other famous novelists are Vennayil Kunniraman Nayanar, Appan Tampuran, V. K. Kunnan Menon, Ambati Narayana Potuval and C. P. Achyuta Menon. Vaikkom Mohammad Bashir is a famous dignitary in the Malayalam Literary scenario. Some famous Malayali poets are Kumaran Ashan, G. Sankara Kurup, K. K. Raja, Channampuzha Krishna Pilla and N. Balamaniyamma. So we see, the Malayalam Language has truly come of age.

LANGUAGE SPOKEN

In Kerala, the inhabitants speak a wide array of languages. Not only these languages are spoken in Kerala but are also taught here. The most widely spoken languages in this state are Malayalam and English. Since people of this place are highly educated and learned, English language is used predominantly in schools and colleges as teaching communication. Beside these two languages, there are many more languages spoken here.

These languages reflect the diverse ethnicities not only in the state but also in the country. The state boasts of contained functioning communities that speak these dialects and languages that are not heard anywhere in the country. About sixteen languages are spoken in Kerala that have been recognized by Kerala State Authorities. The reason behind it is division of this state in terms of religion and culture.

Various Languages

Kerala houses about 225 communities. About 112 communities speak Malayalam language, whereas only one community speaks English language. However, with change, this scenario is also undergoing change and today, English language is majorly used as a means of communication in schools, colleges and other institutions. Other languages that are spoken here are Sanskrit, Talim and Pali that had immense impact on Malayalam language. With some words from Arabic and Urdu, Malayalam language is also spoken by Muslim communities.

Tamil language is also used as a language of conversation by about 39 communities residing in this state. Tamil was the language that was used by Dravidian settlers as a form of expression. The rulers of this place officially recognized Tamil language for communication. Tulu, Telugu and Kannada were the other main languages used in this state. These languages fill the gap of communication.

In comparison to other languages, other languages that are spoken here are Urdu, Marathi, Punjabi, Konkani and Gujarati besides main Keralan communities. Outsiders have introduced these languages in the state that came here and settled here forever. From the communities' names residing in Kerala, other languages among the sixteen languages that inhabitants speak and practice, the names of these languages are adopted.

OFFICIAL LANGUAGE OF KERALA

The officially recognized language spoken in the state of Kerala is Malayalam. This is one of the states in India where the state official language is also the country's official language.

Under India's Dravidian Language Classification, Malayalam language falls. Since the vocabulary has undergone a major change in past years, the dialect that is spoken in Kerala is distinct from the old dialect. Syllabic system of alphabets is followed in the Malayalam language that is spoken today. There are 35 consonants in Malayalam language besides sixteen vowels. There is an alveolar nasal that extends the alphabet count to 52. Quite close to the Tamil script, the language shares a lot of similarities with Malayalam. The main difference is reflected in Malayalam languages' similarity with Sanskrit. This language is considered to be quite refined language.

Influence of Sanskrit language is felt more in Malayalam in comparison to Tamil. Malayalam language is spoken by more than 24,000,000 inhabitants residing in the state of Kerala. It is one of the oldest languages in Kerala as historians have studies inscriptions that have been written in Malayalam language since nineteenth century.

Tourists coming to this state have to face challenge of speaking a language for communication, though English language is not only understood but also spoken by the residents residing in Kerala. But the problem faced is that most of the inhabitants living here refuse to speak any language besides their own language. They prefer only their mother tongue for communication.

The tradition and culture of this state do not encourage use of any other language besides Malayalam. They speak no other language rather than Malayalam with people coming from other parts of the country or the world. As per certain reports, the Malayalam language is used predominantly in educational institutions like schools, colleges and institutes in this state and other state of South India that encompasses Lakshadweep, South Canara, Mahe and Kodagu besides USA or the United States of America. There are several Malayalam language's dialects that teachers in the state of Kerala try hard to teach their students studying in this state as well as abroad. Three dialects of Malayalam are spoken in Kerala that depended on the traditions that were practiced and the region.

PRINCIPAL LANGUAGE

The principal language being used in Kerala is Malayalam. The term 'Malayalam' as referring to the language of Kerala is of comparatively recent origin. To begin with, it denoted the land itself. It is probable that the term is the resultant of a combination of two words, mala meaning mountain and alam meaning the land or locality (which lies along side the mountain). Subsequently the synonyms Malayanma and Malayayma came into being as denoting the language of the Malayalam County and finally the name of the land itself was taken over as the name of its language.

Evidently Malayalam belongs to the Dravidian family of languages, but there is considerable difference of opinion about the exact nature of its relationship with the other languages of the stock, with Tamil in particular towards which it bears the closest affinity. Quite a few scholars are of the opinion that Malayalam is but an offshoot of Tamil, or rather, a daughter. This view, first held by Bishop Caldwell, has since been elaborated and substantiated by a well-known grammarian of Kerala, A.R.Raja Raja Varma. The intimacy that subsisted between the two languages all through the centuries, the identity that the grammars and vocabularies of both the languages evince, and the old practice of using the term 'Tamil' as a synonym for Malayalam have all lent considerable support to this theory. But in the light of the increasing application of scientific methodologies in the assessment of affinities between languages and the comparative studies since carried out in respect of the two languages, this theory would seem to require further examination.

Dialects

Malayalam is classified as a South Dravidian language. It is the official language of Kerala. All Keralites consider Malayalam as their mother tongue. Possessing an independent written script, it also has a rich modern literature. There are at least five main regional dialects of Malayalam and a number of communal dialects. It belongs to the Dravidian family. Many words have been borrowed from Sanskrits. There are 37 consonants and 16 vowels in the script. Malayalam has a written traditional dating back from the late 9th century and the earliest work dates from 13th century. The script used is called Kolezhethu (Rod-script) which is derived from ancient Grandha Script. Malayalam differs from other Dravidian language as the absence of personal endings on verbs. It has a one to one correspondence with the Indo Aryan Devanagari syllabarry.

Alphabets

At present Malayalam has a script of its own, but in the early centuries it used a form called the vattezhuthu which had currency all over the regions of the Cheras and the Pandyas. It disappeared from the rest of the peninsula by about the fifteenth century, but in Kerala it continued to be in use for three more centuries. Documents, letters, books and inscriptions were mostly written in this script, and even after giving it up, children first initiated into the study of the language were required to learn the vattezhuthu characters also, besides those of Malayalam and Tamil.

From the vattezhuthu was derived another script called the kolezhuthu. It is said that the ezhuthu or writing was done with a kol, a stick, and hence the name kolezhuthu for the script. There is no fundamental difference between the two scripts except that in kolezhuthu there are no specific symbols for endings in u and for a and o. This script was more commonly used in the Cochin and Malabar areas than in Travancore. Yet another script derived from the vattezhuthu was the Malayanma, which was in common use to the south of Thiruvananthapuram. Malayanma also does not differ fundamentally from the vattezhuthu.

With three scripts in current use the writing and reading of Malayalam must indeed have been a difficult affair. Vattezhuthu was perhaps the better form, for it had currency all over Kerala and did not have any regional variations. But the absence of character combinations, the vowels a and o and conventions for symbols were real difficulties. The trouble with kolezhuthu was still more considerable, for it knew regional variations also. And in the case Malayanma, the complexity of the script, Tamil usages and conventional abbreviations for words were handicaps which made it unintelligible to the rest of the region. It is likely that in course of time these difficulties contributed to their disappearance and brought in the grandhalipi which is the basis of the present script.

It is held that grandhalipi the term literally means 'book-script' was in use all over South India since the seventh century A.D. The advent of Manipravala literature must have been the major factor that paved the way for its introduction in Kerala.

LITERATURE

Malayalam literature is ancient in origin, and includes such figures as the 14th century Niranam poets (Madhava Panikkar, Sankara Panikkar and Rama Panikkar), whose works mark the dawn of both modern Malayalam language and indigenous Keralite poetry. The Triumvirate of poets (*Kavithrayam*: Kumaran Asan, Vallathol Narayana Menon and Ulloor S. Parameswara Iyer) are recognized for moving keralian poetry away from archaic sophistry and metaphysics and towards a more lyrical mode. Poets like Changampuzha, Cherusseri, Pallathu Raman, and Edappally Raghavan Pillai also contributed to bring Malayalam poetry to the common man. Later, such contemporary writers as Booker Prize winner Arundhati Roy (whose 1996 semi-autobiographical bestseller *The God of Small Things* is set in the Kottayam town of Ayemenem) have garnered international recognition. From 1970 to early 1990s, a lot of Malayalam Novelists and story writers contributed to the Literature of Kerala. The contributions from Thakazhi Sivashankara Pillai, Vaikom Muhammed Basheer P. Kesavadev, Uroob, OV Vijayan, T Padmanabhan, Sethu, Perumbadavam Sreedharan, Kovilan, M. Mukundan, Kakkanadan, Anand and Paul Zacharia, have been remarkable. Significant contributions from poets and songwriters such as Vayalar Rama Varma, P. Bhaskaran and ONV Kurup have influenced contemporary literature. Critics such as Kuttikrishna Marar and M.P. Paul till the sixties and later, M Krishnan Nair, S. Gupthan Nair, M. K. Sanu, Sukumar Azhikode, K.P. Appan, Narendra Prasad and M. Leelavathy have added value by providing critical analysis of the books written during the recent past.

Literature

Malayalam literature starts from the late medieval period and includes such notable writers as the 14th-century Niranam poets (Madhava Panikkar, Sankara Panikkar and Rama Panikkar), and the 17th-century poet Thunchathththu Ezhuthachan, whose works mark the dawn of both the modern Malayalam language and its poetry. Paremmakkal Thoma Kathanar and Kerala Varma Valiakoi Thampuran are noted for their contribution to Malayalam prose. The "triumvirate of poets" (*Kavithrayam*): Kumaran Asan, Vallathol Narayana Menon, and Ulloor S. Parameswara Iyer, are recognised for moving Keralite poetry away from archaic sophistry and metaphysics, and towards a more lyrical mode. In the second half of the 20th century, Jnanpith winning poets and writers like G. Sankara Kurup, S. K. Pottekkatt, Thakazhi Sivasankara Pillai, M. T. Vasudevan Nair and O. N. V. Kurup had made valuable contributions to the modern Malayalam literature. Later, writers like O. V. Vijayan, Kamaladas, M. Mukundan, Arundhati Roy, Vaikom Muhammed Basheer, have gained international recognition.

5

Geography and Flora & Fauna

GEOGRAPHY OF KERALA

Kerala (38,863 km^2; 1.18% of India's landmass) is situated between the Arabian Sea to the west and the Western Ghats to the east. Kerala's coast runs some 580 km in length, while the state itself varies between 35–120 km in width. Geographically, Kerala roughly divides into three climatically distinct regions.

These include the eastern highlands (rugged and cool mountainous terrain), the central midlands (rolling hills), and the western lowlands (coastal plains). Located at the extreme southern tip of the Indian subcontinent, Kerala lies near the center of the Indian tectonic plate (the Indian Plate); as such most of the state (notwithstanding isolated regions) is subject to comparatively little seismic or volcanic activity. Geologically, pre-Cambrian and Pleistocene formations comprise the bulk of Kerala's terrain. The topography consists of a hot and wet coastal plain gradually rising in elevation to the high hills and mountains of the Western Ghats. Kerala lies between north latitudes 8°.17'.30" N and 12°. 47'.40" N and east longitudes 74°.27'47" E and 77°.37'.12" E. Kerala's climate is mainly wet and maritime tropical, heavily influenced by the seasonal heavy rains brought up by the monsoon.

A small mountain stream in the Nelliampathi mountains

Kerala, which lies in the tropic region, is mostly subject to the type of humid tropical wet climate experienced by most of Earth's rainforests.

Meanwhile, its extreme eastern fringes experience a drier tropical wet and dry climate. Kerala receives an average annual rainfall of 3107 mm – some 7,030 crore m^3 of water.

This compares to the all-India average is 1,197 mm. Parts of Kerala's lowlands may average only 1250 mm annually while the cool mountainous eastern highlands of Idukki district – comprising Kerala's wettest region – receive in excess of 5,000 mm of orographic precipitation (4,200 crore of which area available for human use) annually.

Kerala's rains are mostly the result of seasonal monsoons. As a result, Kerala averages some 120–140 rainy days per year.

In summer, most of Kerala is prone to gale-force winds, storm surges, and torrential downpours accompanying dangerous cyclones coming in off the Indian Ocean. Kerala's average maximum daily temperature is around 37 °C; the minimum is 19.8 °C.

Anamudi, on the right, as seen from the Munnar-Udumalpettai highway

Vembanad, the largest lake in Kerala

The state is wedged between the Lakshadweep Sea and the Western Ghats. Lying between northern latitudes 8°18' and

12°48' and eastern longitudes 74°52' and 77°22', Kerala experiences the humid equatorial tropic climate. The state has a coast of 590 km (370 mi) and the width of the state varies between 11 and 121 kilometres (7 and 75 mi).

Geographically, Kerala can be divided into three climatically distinct regions: the eastern highlands; rugged and cool mountainous terrain, the central mid-lands; rolling hills, and the western lowlands; coastal plains.

Pre-Cambrian and Pleistocene geological formations compose the bulk of Kerala's terrain. A catastrophic flood in Kerala in 1341 CE drastically modified its terrain and consequently affected its history; it also created a natural harbour for spice transport.

The eastern region of Kerala consists of high mountains, gorges and deep-cut valleys immediately west of the Western Ghats' rain shadow. 41 of Kerala's west-flowing rivers, and 3 of its east-flowing ones originate in this region. The Western Ghats form a wall of mountains interrupted only near Palakkad; hence also known Pal*ghat*, where the Palakkad Gap breaks. The Western Ghats rise on average to 1,500 metres (4,900 feet) above sea level, while the highest peaks reach around 2,500 metres (8,200 feet).Anamudi in the Idukki district is the highest peak in south India, is at an elevation of 2,695 m (8,842 ft).

Kerala's western coastal belt is relatively flat compared to the eastern region, and is criss-crossed by a network of interconnected brackish canals, lakes, estuaries, and rivers known as the Kerala Backwaters. The state's largest lake Vembanad, dominates the backwaters; it lies between Alappuzha and Kochi and is about 200 km^2 (77 sq mi) in area. Around eight percent of India's waterways are found in Kerala. Kerala's 44 rivers include the Periyar; 244 kilometres (152 mi), Bharathapuzha; 209 kilometres (130 mi), Pamba; 176 kilometres (109 mi), Chaliyar; 169 kilometres (105 mi), Kadalundipuzha; 130 kilometres (81 mi), Chalakudipuzha; 130 kilometres (81 mi), Valapattanam; 129 kilometres (80 mi) and the Achankovil River; 128 kilometres (80 mi). The average length of the rivers is 64 kilometres (40 mi). Many of the rivers are small and entirely fed by monsoon rain. As Kerala's rivers are small and lacking in delta, they are more prone to environmental effects. The rivers face problems such as sand mining and pollution. The state experiences several natural hazards like landslides, floods and droughts. The state was also affected by the 2004 Indian Ocean tsunami, and in 2018 received the worst flooding in nearly a century.

Climate

With around 120–140 rainy days per year, Kerala has a wet and maritime tropical climate influenced by the seasonal heavy rains of the southwest summer monsoon and northeast winter monsoon. Around 65% of the rainfall occurs from June to August corresponding to the Southwest monsoon, and the rest from September to December corresponding to Northeast monsoon. The moisture-laden winds of the Southwest monsoon, on reaching the southernmost point of the Indian Peninsula, because of its topography, divides into two branches; the "Arabian Sea Branch" and the "Bay of Bengal Branch". The "Arabian Sea Branch" of the Southwest monsoon first hits the Western Ghats, making Kerala the first state in India to receive rain from the Southwest monsoon. The distribution of pressure patterns is reversed in the Northeast monsoon, during this season the cold winds from North India pick up moisture from the Bay of Bengal and precipitate it on the east coast of peninsular India. In Kerala, the influence of the Northeast monsoon is seen in southern districts only. Kerala's rainfall averages 2,923 mm (115 in) annually. Some of Kerala's drier lowland regions average only 1,250 mm (49 in); the mountains of the eastern Idukki district receive more than 5,000 mm (197 in) of orographic precipitation: the highest in the state. In eastern Kerala, a drier tropical wet and dry climate prevails. During the summer, the state is prone to gale-force winds, storm surges, cyclone-related torrential downpours, occasional droughts, and rises in sea level. The mean daily temperature ranges from 19.8 °C to 36.7 °C. Mean annual temperatures range from 25.0–27.5 °C in the coastal lowlands to 20.0–22.5 °C in the eastern highlands.

Geography

Eastern Kerala consists of land encroached upon by the Western Ghats; the region thus includes high mountains, gorges, and deep-cut valleys. The wildest lands are covered with dense forests, while other regions lie under tea and coffee plantations (established mainly in the 19th and 20th centuries) or other forms of cultivation. Forty-one of Kerala's forty-four rivers originate in this region, and the Cauvery River descends from there and drains eastwards into neighboring states. Here, the Western Ghats form a wall of mountains penetrated near Palakkad; here, a natural mountain pass known as the Palakkad Gapbreaks through to access inner India. The Western Ghats rises on average to 1500 m elevation above sea level. Certain peaks may reach to 2500 m. Just west of the mountains lie the midland plains, comprising a swathe of land running along central Kerala. Here, rolling hills and shallow valleys fill a gentler landscape than the highlands. In the lowest lands, the midlands region hosts paddy fields; meanwhile, elevated lands slopes play host to groves of rubber and fruit trees in addition to other crops such as black pepper, tapioca, and others.

The lighthouse and beach at Kovalam

Finally, Kerala's coastal belt is relatively flat, teeming with paddy fields, groves of coconut trees, and heavily crisscrossed by a network of interconnected canals and rivers. The comparative water-richness of the coastal belt can be partly gauged by the fact that Kuttanad, with its backwaters canals and rivers, itself comprises more than 20% of India's waterways by length. The most important of Kerala's forty-four rivers include the Periyar (244 km in length), the Bharathapuzha (209 km), the Pamba River (176 km),the chaliyar river(169) the Chalakudy Puzha(144 km), the Kadalundipuzha (130 km), and the Achancoil (128 km). Most of the remainder are small and entirely fed by the Monsoons.

There are 44 rivers in Kerala, all but three originating in the Western Ghats. 41 of them flow westward and 3 eastward. The rivers of Kerala are small, in terms of length, breadth and water discharge. The rivers flow faster, owing to the hilly terrain and as the short distance between the Western Ghats and the sea. All the rivers are entirely monsoon-fed and many of them shrink into rivulets or dry up completely during summer.

Estuary in Thekkumbhagam, Paravur

The Kerala Backwaters region is a particularly well-recognized feature of Kerala; it is an interconnected system of brackish water lakes and river estuariesthat lies inland from the coast and runs virtually the length of the state. These facilitate inland travel throughout a region roughly bounded by Thiruvananthapuram in the south and Vatakara (which lies some 450 km to the north). There are 34 backwaters in Kerala Lake Vembanad—Kerala's largest body of water —dominates the backwaters; it lies between Alappuzha and Kochi and is over 200 km^2 in area. Major lakes of Kerala include:

Mountains

The Western Ghats is a continuous mountain range of 450 km along the eastern side of Kerala. It forms almost an unbroken wall guarding the eastern frontier and helps the people of Kerala to lead a sheltered life of their own through the centuries. The Western Ghats is also responsible for the high and steady rainfall in Kerala. It converts 50% of Kerala into highlands and is studded with more than 50 peaks above 5000 feet above Mean Sea Level. With a height of 8841 feet (2,695 metres), Anamudi is the highest peak in India outside Himalayas.

Natural Hazards in Kerala

Kerala is prone to several natural hazards, the most common of them being landslides, flooding, lightning, drought, coastal erosion, earthquakes, Tsunami, wind fall and epidemics.

Landslides

The highlands of Kerala experience several types of landslides, of which debris flows are the most common. They are called 'Urul Pottal' in the local vernacular. The characteristic pattern of this phenomenon is the swift and sudden downslope movement of highly water saturated overburden containing a varied assemblage of debris material ranging in size from soil particles to boulders, destroying and carrying with it every thing that is lying in its path. The west facing Western Ghats scarps that runs the entire extent of the mountain system is the most prone physiographic unit for landslides. These scarp faces are characterised by thin soil (regolith) cover modified heavily by anthropogenic activity. The highlands of the region experience an annual average rainfall as high as 500 cm from the South-West, North-East and Pre-Monsoon showers. A review of ancient documents, investigation reports and news paper reports indicates a lesser rate of slope instability in the past; 29 major landslide events that occurred in the recent past was identified through the review. The processes leading to landslides were accelerated by anthropogenic disturbances such as deforestation since the early 18th century, terracing and obstruction of ephemeral streams and cultivation of crops lacking capability to add root cohesion in steep slopes. The events have become more destructive given the increasing vulnerability of population and property. Majority of mass movements have occurred in hill slopes >20° along the Western Ghats scarps, the only exception being the coastal cliffs. Studies conducted in the state indicates that prolonged and intense rainfall or more particularly a combination of the two and the resultant persistence and variations of pore pressure are the most important trigger of landslides. The initiation of most of the landslides were in typical hollows generally having degraded natural vegetation. All except 1 of the 14 districts in the state are prone to landslides. Wayanad and Kozhikode districts are prone to deep seated landslides while Idukki and Kottayam are prone to shallow landslides. A very recent study indicates that the additional cohesion provided by vegetation roots in soil is an important contributor to slope stability in the scarp faces of the Western Ghats of Kerala.

Flooding

Although the Kerala state does not experience floods as severe as in the Indo-Gangetic plains, incidence of floods in the State is becoming more frequent and severe. The latest among them was the 2018 Kerala floods. Continuous occurrence of high intensity rainfall for a few days is the primary factor contributing to the extreme floods in the State. Other factors include wrong landuse practices and mismanagement of the water resources and forests. The human interventions contributing to flood problems are predominantly in the form of reclamation of wetlands and water bodies, change in landuse pattern, construction of dense networks of roads, establishment of more and more settlements, deforestation in the upper catchments etc. Increasing floodplain occupancy results in increasing flood damages. A number of extreme flood events occurred during the last century causing considerable damage to life and property highlight the necessity for proper flood management measures in the State. The flood problems are likely to worsen with the continued floodplain occupancy and reclamation of water bodies and wetlands. It is estimated that about 25% of the total geographical area accommodating about 18% of the total population of the State is prone to floods.

Lightning

Kerala is a place of high lightning incidence compared to most of the other parts in India because of its weather patterns and the location of the Western Ghats. Higher population density and vegetation density result in more casualties. Lack of awareness also aggravates the situation. Accidents caused by ground conduction from trees, which is a special feature of Kerala, add to the casualties and loss of property. The records show that the months April, May, October and November have the highest lightning rates. The most active time of the day is from 15:00 to 19:00. Of the fourteen districts, five have much higher rates than others. The severe impact of the hazard on the state and its people is seen from the very high average casualty rates of 71 deaths, 112 injuries and 188 accidents per annum. Losses to telephone communications, networked systems and electrical equipment are also very high.

Drought

Kerala has been experiencing increasing incidents of drought in the recent past due to the weather anomalies and developmental pressures resulting from the changes in land use, traditional practices, and life style of the people. The increase in population and subsequent expansion in irrigated agriculture, and industrial growth necessitated the exploitation of more water resources. The changes in the land and water management practices affected the fresh water availability during summer months. Although the deviation in the annual rainfall received in Kerala, in any year from the long term average is very small, there is considerable variation in the rainfall availability during the different seasons.

About 95 percent of annual rainfall is confined to a six-month monsoon period between June and November, leaving the remaining six months as practically dry. Soman (1988) reported that over major part of the Kerala State, extreme as well as these where the rainfall is more compared to other areas. The changes in rainfall pattern may have association with the environmental modifications due to human interventions on the natural ecosystems.

The State of Kerala experiences seasonal drought conditions every year during the summer months. Even in the years of normal rainfall, summer water scarcity problems are severe in the midland and highland regions. Severe drought conditions often result from the anomalies in monsoon rainfall combined with the various anthropogenic pressures.

A study on the incidence of droughts based on the aridity index shows that during the period 1871– 2000, the State of Kerala experienced 66 drought years, out of which, twelve each were moderate and severe droughts. The droughts have a large dimension of economic, environmental and social impacts. With the implementation of a number of irrigation projects, the idea of drought in Kerala slowly shifted to unirrigated paddy, and upland crops. The water scarcity in summer is mainly reflected in dry rivers and lowering of water table. This adversely affects the rural and urban drinking water supply. As seen in the majority of drought incidents, even a 20% fall in the northeast monsoon, can make the water scarcity situation worse during the summer. Since the State has more of perennial plantation crops compared to other places of India, the effect of a drought year in Kerala continues to be felt for several more years after it has occurred. Thus, for better planning of the drought management measures, the term drought with reference to plantation crops should be redefined based on rainfall received or available soil moisture during summer months instead of total monsoon rainfall.

Tsunami

The Kerala coast was significantly affected by the 2004 Indian Ocean tsunami. The coast located in the shadow zone with respect to the direction of propagation of the tsunami encountered unexpected devastation. Although the tsunami affected parts of Kerala coast, maximum devastation was reported in the low coastal land of Kollam, Alappuzha and Ernakulam districts, particularly a strip of 10 km in Azhikkal, Kollam district.

This varying effect along the coast could be attributed to local amplification of tsunami waves in certain regions. About 176 people were killed and 1600 injured in the coastal belt. Further, the tsunami pounded 187 villages affecting nearly 250,000 persons in Kerala. As many as 6,280 dwelling units were completely destroyed, 11,175 were damaged and nearly 84,773 persons were evacuated from the coastal areas and accommodated in 142 relief camps after tsunami. As this tsunami is believed to be first of its kind to have significantly affected the Kerala coast, the post-tsunami field investigations and measurements would give valuable information on various changes brought by the tsunami. Immediately after the tsunami, several organizations have carried out field surveys in many affected areas along the coast.

Geography education in Kerala

Undergraduate and Masters level education is offered in the Universities of Kerala. Research in Geography is carried out in a variety of organizations like Department of Geography, University College, National Centre for Earth Sciences Studies, Kannur University etc.

WILDLIFE OF KERALA

Most of Kerala, whose native habitat consists of wet evergreen rainforests at lower elevations and highland deciduous and semi-evergreenforests in the east, is subject to a humid tropical climate. however, significant variations in terrain and elevation have resulted in a land whose biodiversity registers as among the world's most significant.

A great hornbill (Buceros bicornis) as pictured in a German zoo

Evergreen forests

Most of Kerala's significantly biodiverse tracts of wilderness lie in the evergreen forests of its easternmost districts; coastal Kerala (along with portions of the east) mostly lies under cultivation and is home to comparatively little wildlife. Despite this, Kerala contains 9,400 km^2 of natural forests. Out of the approximately 7,500 km^2 of non-plantation forest cover, there are wild regions of tropical wet evergreen and semi-evergreen forests (lower and middle elevations — 3,470 km^2), tropical moist and dry deciduous forests (mid-elevations — 4,100 km^2

and 100 km^2, respectively), and montane subtropical and temperate (*shola*) forests (highest elevations — 100 km^2). Such forests together cover 24% of Kerala's landmass. Kerala also hosts two of the world's Ramsar Convention-listed wetlands: Lake Sasthamkotta and the Vembanad-Kol wetlands are noted as being wetlands of international importance. There are also numerous protected conservation areas, including 1455.4 km^2 of the vast Nilgiri Biosphere Reserve.

*Figs (*Ficus *species) like this strangler fig are an important floral element and support many frugivores*

Rain Forests

Eastern Kerala's windward mountains shelter tropical moist forests and tropical dry forests which are generally characteristic of the wider Western Ghats: crowns of giant *sonokeling* (binomial nomenclature: *Dalbergia latifolia* — Indian rosewood), *anjili* (*Artocarpus hirsuta*), *mullumurikku* (*Erythrina*), *Cassia*, and other trees dominate the canopies of large tracts of virgin forest.

Overall, Kerala's forests are home to more than 1,000 species of trees. Smaller flora include bamboo, wild black pepper (*Piper nigrum*), wild cardamom, the calamus rattan palm (*Calamus rotang* — a type of giant grass), and aromatic Vetiver grass (*Vetiveria zizanioides*).

Fauna of Kerala

In turn, the forests play host to such major fauna as the Asian elephant (*Elephas maximus*), Bengal tiger (*Panthera tigris tigris*), leopard(*Panthera pardus*), nilgiri tahr (*Nilgiritragus hylocrius*), and grizzled giant squirrel (*Ratufa macroura*).

More remote preserves, including Silent Valley National Park in the Kundali Hills, harbor endangered species such as the Lion-tailed macaque (*Macaca silenus*), Indian sloth bear (*Melursus (Ursus) ursinus ursinus*), and gaur (the so-called "Indian bison" — *Bos gaurus*). More common species include the Indian porcupine (*Hystrix indica*), chital (*Axis axis*), sambar (*Cervus unicolor*), gray langur, flying squirrel, swamp lynx (*Felis chaus kutas*), boar (*Sus scrofa*), a variety of catarrhine Old World monkey species, the gray wolf (*Canis lupus*), and the common palm civet (*Paradoxurus hermaphroditus*).

The king cobra (**Ophiophagus hannah**)

Reptiles

Many reptiles, such as tree snake, green snake, king cobra, viper, python, and various turtles and crocodiles are to be found in Kerala — again, disproportionately in the east.

Kerala has about 453 species of birds such as the Sri Lanka frogmouth (*Batrachostomus moniliger*), leaf picking bird, Oriental bay owl, large frugivores like the great hornbill (*Buceros bicornis*) and Indian grey hornbill, as well as the more widespread birds such as peafowl, Indian cormorant, jungle and hill mynas, the Oriental darter, black-hooded oriole, greater racket-tailed and black drongoes, bulbul (*Pycnonotidae*), species of kingfisher and woodpecker, jungle fowl, Alexandrine parakeets, and assorted ducks and migratory birds.

Additionally, freshwater fish such as *kadu* (stinging catfish — *Heteropneustes fossilis*) and brackishwater species such as *Choottachi* (orange chromide — *Etroplus maculatus*; valued as an aquarium specimen) also are native to Kerala's lakes and waterways.

The Nilgiri tahr, spotted in the Eravikulam National Park in IdukkiDistrict

National park	Area (km^2)	Year started
Eravikulam National Park	97	1978
Periyar National Park	350	1982
Silent Valley National Park	237. 52	1984
Anamudi Shola National Park	7.5	2003
Mathikettan Shola National Park	12.817	2003
Pambadum Shola National Park	1.318	2003
Biosphere Reserve	Area (km^2)	Year started
Nilgiri Biosphere Reserve	1455.4	1986
Agasthyamalai Biosphere Reserve	1701	2002
Wildlife sanctuary	**Area (km^2)**	**Year started**
Periyar Wildlife Sanctuary	777	1950
Neyyar Wildlife Sanctuary	128	1958
Peechi-Vazhani Wildlife Sanctuary	125	1958
Wayanad Wildlife Sanctuary	344.44	1973
Parambikulam Wildlife Sanctuary	285	1973
Idukki Wildlife Sanctuary	70	1976
Thattekad Bird Sanctuary	25	1983
Peppara Wildlife Sanctuary	53	1983
Chimmony Wildlife sanctuary	85	1984
Chinnar Wildlife Sanctuary	90.44	1984
Shendurney Wildlife Sanctuary	171	1984
Aralam Wildlife Sanctuary	55	1984
Mangalavanam Bird Sanctuary	0.0274	2004
Kurinjimala Sanctuary	32	2006
Tiger reserve	**Area (km^2)**	**Year started**
Periyar Tiger Reserve	925	1978
Parambikulam Tiger Reserve	648.50	1973

FLORA AND FAUNA OF KERALA

Flora and Fauna of Kerala are diverse. The favourable climate with heavy rainfall and good quality of the soils helps both the flora and fauna to thrive. Forest covers a large area in the Western Ghats of Kerala.

Flora and Fauna of Kerala are hugely supported by the rich soil, heavy rainfall and damp climate. All these factors have given rise to a diverse variety of flora in the region. Forest area is largely spread over the Western Ghats. The Western Ghats represent one of the 18 hot spots of bio-diversity of the world and is considered to be a depositary of endemic, rare and endangered flora and fauna. Forest trees can be broadly classified as timber trees and flower trees. Teak tree, rosewood and ebony are the most important in the first category. Among the flowering trees, the more important are the Barringtonia and varieties of Bauhinia and Hibiscus. Jack Fruit Tree and mango tree are found almost in all the regions of the state.

The recorded forest area of Kerala is 11,125.59 sq km. This includes 9157.10 sq km reserve forests; 214.31 sq km proposed reserve and 1754.18 sq. km vested forest. Out of the total of 11,125 sq km of recorded forest area, the effective (actual) forest area in Kerala is only 9400 sq km. The forests in the state can be divided into seven major types, which are subdivided into many sub-types depending upon the floristic composition and site factors. According to this classification, there are 28 vegetation types in the state of Kerala.

Besides the flora, Kerala's fauna is varied too. The forests are abounding in elephants, black leopards, tigers, sloth bears, giant squirrels and a variety of deer. The delightful specimens of the bird life include the charming little honey-sucker with glorious metallic colours, the golden-backed woodpecker, the little white-eyed tit which creeps among the leaves, and the Malabar whistling thrush which has earned the name 'Drunken

Plough Boy' by its musical exertions. The area is covered by the two national parks, twelve wild life sanctuaries and one biosphere coming under the category of protected areas in Kerala. It is near about 2.32 lakh hectares. It is around 25 per cent of the total area under forests and around six per cent of the total geographical area, which is higher than the national average of five per cent. Protected areas showcase the bio-diversity of Kerala.

Flora and Fauna Of Kerala

The southernmost Indian state, Kerala, is known for its scenic beauty and green ambience. The green rich landscape of this destination also blessed with a wide range of flora and fauna. The natural habitat of the state makes it a haven for different animal and bird species. The landscape of Kerala encompasses highland deciduous, evergreen forests and partially evergreen forests in different parts of the state. Besides, this destination has humid tropical climate due its unique terrain and elevation. These unique features of Kerala make it the land of highly important biodiversity in the world. Explore the exotic flora and fauna of the state through KSU. Log on our website www.ksu.in to get an idea about the different plants and animals in the state.

Flora and fauna

Most of the biodiversity is concentrated and protected in the Western Ghats. Three quarters of the land area of Kerala was under thick forest up to 18th century. As of 2004, over 25% of India's 15,000 plant species are in Kerala. Out of the 4,000 flowering plantspecies; 1,272 of which are endemic to Kerala, 900 are medicinal, and 159 are threatened. Its 9,400 km^2 of forests include tropical wet evergreen and semi-evergreen forests (lower and middle elevations—3,470 km^2), tropical moist and dry deciduous forests (mid-elevations—4,100 km^2 and 100 km^2, respectively), and montane subtropical and temperate (*shola*) forests (highest elevations—100 km^2). Altogether, 24% of Kerala is forested. Three of the world's Ramsar Convention listed wetlands—Lake Sasthamkotta, Ashtamudi Lake and the

Vembanad-Kol wetlands—are in Kerala, as well as 1455.4 km^2 of the vast Nilgiri Biosphere Reserve. Subjected to extensive clearing for cultivation in the 20th century, much of the remaining forest cover is now protected from clearfelling. Eastern Kerala's windward mountains shelter tropical moist forests and tropical dry forests, which are common in the Western Ghats. The world's oldest teak plantation 'Conolly's Plot' is in Nilambur.

Kerala's fauna are notable for their diversity and high rates of endemism: it includes 118 species of mammals (1 endemic), 500 species of birds, 189 species of freshwater fish, 173 species of reptiles (10 of them endemic), and 151 species of amphibians (36 endemic).These are threatened by extensive habitat destruction, including soil erosion, landslides, salinisation, and resource extraction. In the forests, *sonokeling*, *Dalbergia latifolia*, *anjili*, *mullumurikku*, *Erythrina*, and *Cassia* number among the more than 1,000 species of trees in Kerala. Other plants include bamboo, wild black pepper, wild cardamom, the calamus rattan palm, and aromatic vetiver grass, *Vetiveria zizanioides*. Indian elephant, Bengal tiger, Indian leopard, Nilgiri tahr, common palm civet, and grizzled giant squirrelsare also found in the forests. Reptiles include the king cobra, viper, python, and mugger crocodile. Kerala's birds include the Malabar trogon, the great hornbill, Kerala laughingthrush, darter and southern hill myna. In the lakes, wetlands, and waterways, fish such as *kadu*; stinging catfish and *choottachi*; orange chromide—*Etroplus maculatus* are found.

Nilgiri tahr

Indian giant squirrel, Silent Valley National Park

Elephants at Thekkady

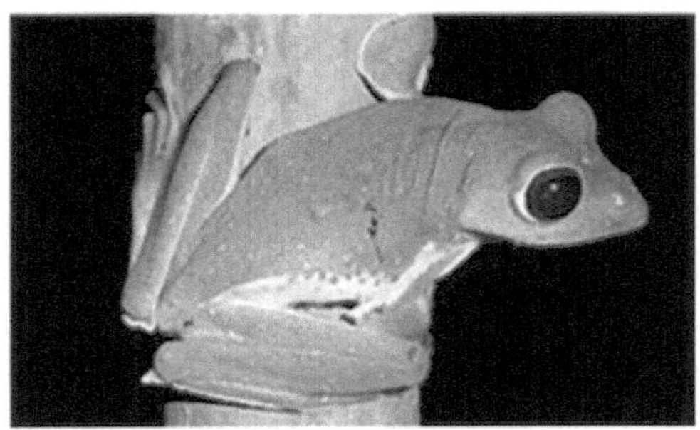

Rhacophorus malabaricus

Brahminy kite

Lesser golden-backed woodpecker

Subdivisions

The state's 14 districts are distributed among six regions: North Malabar (far-north Kerala), South Malabar (northern Kerala), Kochi (central Kerala), Northern Travancore, Central Travancore (southern Kerala) and Southern Travancore (far-south Kerala). The districts which serve as administrative regions for taxation purposes are further subdivided into 75 taluks, which have fiscal and administrative powers over settlements within their borders, including maintenance of local land records. Kerala's taluks are further sub-divided into 1,453 revenue villages. Since the 73rd and 74th amendments to the Constitution of India, the local government institutions function as the third tier of government, which constitutes 14

District Panchayats, 152 Block Panchayats, 978 Grama Panchayats, 60 Municipalities, six Corporations and one Township. Mahé, a part of the Indian union territory of Puducherry, though 647 kilometres (402 mi) away from it, is a coastal exclave surrounded by Kerala on all of its landward approaches. The Kannur District surrounds Mahé on three sides with the Kozhikode District on the fourth.

There are six Municipal corporations in Kerala that govern Thiruvananthapuram, Kollam, Kochi, Thrissur, Kozhikode and Kannur. The Thiruvananthapuram Municipal Corporation is the largest corporation in Kerala while Kochi metropolitan area named Kochi UA is the largest urban agglomeration. According to a survey by economics research firm Indicus Analytics in 2007, Thiruvananthapuram, Kollam, Kozhikode, Thrissur, Kochi and Kannur are among the "best cities in India to live"; the survey used parameters such as health, education, environment, safety, public facilities and entertainment to rank the cities.

A STATE WITH NATURAL FORESTS

The major biodiversity area of Kerala lies in the middle of the evergreen forests particularly in the eastern districts of the state. Some of the coastal areas of this state also occupy such biodiversity tracts. Since most of the regions in this part are under cultivation, not much wildlife registered at the coastal areas. Kerala has more than 9000 sq. km of natural forests out of which nearly 7500 sq km comes under the non-plantation area. Approximately 3400 sq. km area covers both wet evergreen and semi evergreen forests. Nearly 100 sq km areas of this state cover dry deciduous forests while the moist tropical region sprawled in an area of almost 4000 sq. km.

Kerala is also famous for Shola forests and nearly 24% of the area of this state is covered by such forests. It can be seen mainly at the high elevated areas of the state. There are two wetland areas in the state, Vembanad-Kol and Lake Sasthamkotta. Both of them are considered to be listed in the famous Ramsar Convention. Above all, Kerala has several protected areas including the well known Nilgiri Biosphere Reserve.

Flora

The windward mountain regions situated to the eastern part of Kerala covers moist and tropical dry forests. It is also a part of Western Ghats and famous for its rich flora including anjili, mullumurikku, sonokeling (Indian Rosewood) and Cassia. With more than thousand species of trees, this area has a dense cover. Some of the common flora in this region includes bamboo, palm, wild cardamom, black pepper and Vetiver Grass with amazing aroma.

Fauna

Just like its flora, Kerala is also famous for its rich fauna.

Mammals

This South Indian state is blessed with a wide array of mammals such as Asian Elephant, leopard, Bengal Tiger and Grizzleed Giant Squirrel. The Silent Valley is a famous national park in the state which is located in the Kundali Hills. It houses many endangered species such as Indian Bison, Indian Sloth bear, Lion tailed Macaque etc. Some of the common mammal species registered in Kerala is Indian Porcupine, Flying Squirrel, Swamp Lynx, Common Palm Civet, boar and some species of monkeys.

Reptiles

Kerala is home to a wide range of reptiles and some of the common reptiles registered in this state include King cobra, python, viper, crocodiles and species of turtles.

Avians

Kerala is a paradise for birdwatchers because of the wide range of bird species available in the state. This scenic destination is blessed with nearly 453 species of birds. You can easily watch them by planning a walking tour through the popular bird sanctuaries in Kerala. Some of the avian species that you can spot in these sanctuaries include the Great Hornbill (Zoological Name- Buceros bicornis), are Oriental Bay Owl, Kingfisher, Woodpecker, Sri Lanka Frogmouth (Zoological Name-

Batrachostomus moniliger), Jungle Fowl, Peafowl, Hill Mayna, Indian Cormorant, Black hooded Oriole, Bulbul (Zoological Name-Pycnnotidae), Alexandrine Parakeet and Black Drongoes, You can also see some species of ducks in this state.

Aquatic Species

With numerous rivers, lakes, sea and ponds, Kerala is rich in aquatic species. The backwaters of the state have some freshwater fish. A stinging fish named Kadu is also seen in it. A brackish water species named choottachi is also registered in this state. In addition, many aquatic species are natives of the lakes and waterways of Kerala.

Preservation Of Flora And Fauna

Although Kerala is a small Indian state, it boasts exotic species of flora and fauna. However, unplanned urbanization depletes the rich forest reserve of the state. After realizing the possible repercussions of this situation, the government announced several wildlife sanctuaries and national parks for the preservation of the flora and fauna. Some of the popular wildlife sanctuaries in the state are Periyar Wildlife sanctuary, Neyyar wildlife sanctuary, Peppara Sanctuary, Thattekad Bird Sanctuary and Aralam wildlife sanctuary. The two national parks in the state are Eravikulam National Park and Silent Valley National Park.

6

Economy

ECONOMY OF KERALA

Kerala has the eight largest economy in India. Service industry dominates the Kerala economy. Kerala's per capita GDP in 2016-17 was Rs.140,107. Kerala's high GDP and productivity figures with higher development figures is often dubbed the "Kerala Phenomenon" or the "Kerala Model" of development by economists, political scientists, and sociologists. This phenomenon arises mainly from Kerala's land reforms, social upliftment of entire communities implemented by various governments ruled the state. Some describe Kerala's economy as a "democratic socialist welfare state". Some, such as Financial Express, use the term "Money Order Economy". Kerala's economic progress is above the national average, with numerous major corporations and manufacturing plants being headquartered in Kerala, specifically at Kochi. Estimates of the 2013 Tendulkar Committee Report on poverty suggest that percentages of population below poverty line in rural and urban Kerala are 9.14% and 4.97%

Around 3,000,000 Keralites are working abroad, mainly in Persian Gulf; to where migration started with the Gulf Boom. The Kerala Economy is therefore largely dependent on trade in services and resulted remittances. In 2012, the state was the highest receiver of overall remittances to India which stood at Rs.49,965 Crore (31.2% of the State's GDP), followed by Tamil

Nadu, Punjab and Uttar Pradesh. S. Irudaya Rajan describes the situation as "Remittances from global capitalism are carrying the whole Kerala economy". With 11.8% of the labour force unemployed in 2015, Kerala is 11th in unemployment in India. Underemployment, low employability of youths, and a 13.5% female participation rate are chronic issues. The 'Report on Fifth Annual Employment - Unemployment Survey for 2015-16' prepared by the labour bureau of the Union ministry of labour and employment indicates that Tripura had the highest unemployment rate of 19.7% in India, followed by Sikkim (18.1%) and Kerala (12.5%).

Macro-economic trend

This is a chart of trend of gross state domestic product of Kerala at market prices estimated by *Ministry of Statistics and Programme Implementation* with figures in millions of Indian Rupees.Kerala had recorded a growth rate of 6.49 per cent in 2013, which was above the national average (4.04) and the second highest among South Indian States. The state's growth rate was above that of Karnataka (5.79 per cent) and Andhra Pradesh (5.97 per cent).

Year	Gross State Domestic Product
1980	42,860
1985	75,200
1990	140,980
1995	387,620
2000	697,920
2005	1,025,080

The state's debt was estimated at 29.53 per cent of GDP in 2013. State's debt liability recorded an increase of 14.4 per cent and rose from Rs 1,24,081 crore in 2013-14 to Rs 1,41,947 crore in 2014-15. This liability as a percentage of GSDP was 31.4 per cent, which is higher than the target of 29.8 per cent fixed in the Kerala Fiscal Responsibility Act.The GDP growth rate that continuously stood above the national average, began to show a declining trend from 2012-13, and it further slid to

8.59% in 2015-16, when the national average stood at 9.94%. The tax growth rate, which was 23.24% in 2010-11, fell to 10.68% in 2015-16.

Economy

After independence, the state was managed as a democratic socialist welfare economy. From the 1990s, liberalisation of the mixed economy allowed onerous Licence Rajrestrictions against capitalism and foreign direct investment to be lightened, leading to economic expansion and an increase in employment. In the fiscal year 2007–2008, the nominal gross state domestic product (GSDP) was 1,624 billion (US$23 billion). GSDP growth; 9.2% in 2004–2005 and 7.4% in 2003–2004 had been high compared to an average of 2.3% annually in the 1980s and between 5.1% and 5.99% in the 1990s. The state recorded 8.93% growth in enterprises from 1998 to 2005, higher than the national rate of 4.80%. The "Kerala phenomenon" or "Kerala model of development" of very high human development and in comparison low economic development has resulted from a strong service sector.

Kerala's economy depends on emigrants working in foreign countries, mainly in Arab states of the Persian Gulf, and remittances annually contribute more than a fifth of GSDP.The state witnessed significant emigration during the Gulf Boom of the 1970s and early 1980s. In 2008, the Persian Gulf countries together had a Keralite population of more than 2.5 million, who sent home annually a sum of US$6.81 billion, which is the highest among Indian states and more than 15.13% of remittances to India in 2008. In 2012, Kerala still received the highest remittances of all states: US$11.3 billion, which was nearly 16% of the US$71 billion remittances to the country. In 2015, NRI deposits in Kerala have soared to over 1 lakh crore (US$14 billion), amounting to one-sixth of all the money deposited in NRI accounts, which comes to about 7 lakh crore (US$97 billion). However, a study commissioned by the Kerala State Planning Board, suggested that the state look for other reliable sources of income, instead of relying on remittances to finance its expenditure. According to a study done in 2013, 17,500 crore (US$2.4 billion) was the total amount paid to migrant labourers in the state every year.

Rural women processing coir threads

Common Landscape in every district

The tertiary sector comprises services such as transport, storage, communications, tourism, banking, insurance and real estate. In 2011–2012, it contributed 63.22% of the state's GDP, agriculture and allied sectors contributed 15.73%, while manufacturing, construction and utilities contributed 21.05%. Nearly half of Kerala's people depend on agriculture alone for income. Around 600 varieties of rice, which is Kerala's most used staple and cereal crop, are harvested from 3105.21 km; a decline from 5883.4 km in 1990. 688,859 tonnes of rice are produced per year. Other key crops include coconut; 899,198 ha, tea, coffee; 23% of Indian production, or 57,000 tonnes, rubber, cashews, and spices—including pepper, cardamom, vanilla, cinnamon, and nutmeg.

Traditional industries manufacturing items; coir, handlooms, and handicrafts employ around one million people. Kerala supplies 60% of the total global produce of white coir fibre. India's first coir factory was set up in Alleppey in 1859–60. The Central Coir Research Institute was established there in 1959. As per the 2006–2007 census by SIDBI, there are 1,468,104 micro, small and medium enterprises in Kerala employing 3,031,272 people. The KSIDC has promoted more than 650 medium and large manufacturing firms in Kerala, creating employment for 72,500 people. A mining sector of 0.3% of GSDP involves extraction of ilmenite, kaolin, bauxite, silica, quartz, rutile, zircon, and sillimanite. Other major sectors are tourism, manufacturing, home gardens, animal husbandry and business process outsourcing.

As of March 2002, Kerala's banking sector comprised 3341 local branches: each branch served 10,000 people, lower than the national average of 16,000; the state has the third-highest bank penetration among Indian states. On 1 October 2011, Kerala became the first state in the country to have at least one banking facility in every village. Unemployment in 2007 was estimated at 9.4%; chronic issues are underemployment, low employability of youth, and a low female labour participation rate of only 13.5%, as was the practice of Nokku kooli, "wages for looking on". (On 30 April 2018, the Kerala state government issued an order to abolish nokku kooli, to take effect on 1 May.) By 1999–2000, the rural and urban poverty rates dropped to 10.0% and 9.6% respectively.

Kerala has focused more attention towards growth of Information Technology sector with formation of Technopark, Thiruvananthapuram which is one of the largest IT employer in Kerala. It was the first technology park in India and with the inauguration of the Thejaswini complex on 22 February 2007,

Technopark became the largest IT Park in India. Software giants like Infosys, Oracle, Tata Consultancy Services, Capgemini, HCL, UST Global, Nest and Suntec have offices in the state. The state has a second major IT hub, the Infopark centred in Kochi with "spokes"(it acts as the "hub") in Thrissur and Alleppy. As of 2014, Infopark generates one-third of total IT Revenues of the state with key offices of IT majors like Tata Consultancy Services, Cognizant, Wipro, UST Global, IBS Software Services etc. and Multinational corporations like KPMG, Ernst & Young, EXL Service, Etisalat DB Telecom, Nielsen Audio, Xerox ACS, Tata ELXSI etc. Kochi also has another major project SmartCity under construction, built in partnership with Dubai Government. A third major IT Hub is under construction centred around Kozhikode known as Cyberpark.

The Grand Kerala Shopping Festival (GKSF) was started in 2007, covering more than 3000 outlets across the nine cities of Kerala with huge tax discounts, VAT refunds and huge array of prizes.

Coconut palms can be found all over Kerala

The state's budget of 2012–2013 was 481.42 billion (US$6.7 billion). The state government's tax revenues (excluding the shares from Union tax pool) amounted to 217.22 billion (US$3.0 billion) in 2010–2011; up from 176.25 billion (US$2.5 billion) in 2009–2010. Its non-tax revenues (excluding the shares from Union tax pool) of the Government of Kerala reached 19,308 million (US$270 million) in 2010–2011. However, Kerala's high ratio of taxation to GSDP has not alleviated chronic budget deficits and unsustainable levels of government debt, which have impacted social services. A record total of 223 hartals were observed in 2006, resulting in a revenue loss of over 20 billion (US$280 million). Kerala's 10% rise in GDP is 3% more than the national GDP. In 2013, capital expenditure rose 30% compared to the national average of 5%, owners of two-wheelers rose by 35% compared to the national rate of 15%, and the teacher-pupil ratio rose 50% from 2:100 to 4:100.

In November 2015, the Ministry of Urban Development selected seven cities of Kerala for a comprehensive development program known as the Atal Mission for Rejuvenation and Urban Transformation (AMRUT). A package of 25 lakh (US$35,000) was declared for each of the cities to develop service level improvement plan (SLIP), a plan for better functioning of the local urban bodies in the cities of Thiruvananthapuram, Kollam, Alappuzha, Kochi, Thrissur, Kozhikode, and Palakkad.

Agriculture

Cashew packets displayed in a supermarket. Kollam is a major exporter of cashews.

The major change in agriculture in Kerala occurred in the 1970s when production of rice fell due to increased availability of rice all over India and decreased availability of labour. Consequently, investment in rice production decreased and a major portion of the land shifted to the cultivation of perennial tree crops and seasonal crops. Profitability of crops fell due to a shortage of farm labour, the high price of land, and the uneconomic size of operational holdings.

Kerala produces 97% of the national output of black pepper and accounts for 85% of the natural rubber in the country. Coconut, tea, coffee, cashew, and spices—including cardamom, vanilla, cinnamon, and nutmeg are the main agricultural products. 80% of India's export quality cashew kernels are prepared in Kollam. The key agricultural staple is rice, with varieties grown in extensive paddy fields. Home gardens made up a significant portion of the agricultural sector. Related animal husbandry is touted by proponents as a means of alleviating rural poverty and unemployment among women, the marginalised, and the landless. The state government promotes these activities via educational campaigns and the development of new cattle breeds such as the Sunandini.

A paddy field in Kerala. Rice is the staple crop of the state.

Though the contribution of agricultural sector to the state economy was on the decline in 2012–13, through the strength of the allied livestock sector, it has picked up from 7.03% (2011–12) to 7.2%. In the 2013–14 fiscal period, the contribution has been estimated at a high of 7.75%. The total growth of the farm sector has recorded a 4.39% increase in 2012–13, over a paltry 1.3% growth in the previous fiscal year. The agricultural sector has a share of 9.34% in the sectoral distribution of Gross State Domestic Product at Constant Price, while the secondary and tertiary sectors has contributed 23.94% and 66.72% respectively.

There is a preference for organic products and home farming compared to synthetic fertilizers and pesticides.

Fisheries

Cheena vala (Chinese fishing net)

With 590 kilometres (370 miles) of coastal belt, 400,000 hectares of inland water resources and approximately 220,000 active fishermen, Kerala is one of the leading producers of fish in India.

According to 2003–04 reports, about 1.1 million people earn their livelihood from fishing and allied activities such as drying, processing, packaging, exporting and transporting fisheries. The annual yield of the sector was estimated as 608,000 tons in 2003–04.

This contributes to about 3% of the total economy of the state. In 2006, around 22% of the total Indian marine fishery yield was from Kerala. During the southwest monsoon, a suspended mud bank develops along the shore, which in turn leads to calm ocean water, peaking the output of the fishing industry. This phenomenon is locally called *chakara*.The waters provide a large variety of fish: pelagic species; 59%, demersal species; 23%, crustaceans, molluscs and others for 18%.Around 1.050 million fishermen haul an annual catch of 668,000 tonnes as of a 1999–2000 estimate; 222 fishing villages are strung along the 590-kilometre (370-mile) coast.

Another 113 fishing villages dot the hinterland. Kerala's coastal belt of Karunagappally is known for high background radiation from thorium-containing monazite sand. In some coastal panchayats, median outdoor radiation levels are more than 4 mGy/yr and, in certain locations on the coast, it is as high as 70 mGy/yr.

TRANSPORT

The main Portico of the Thiruvananthapuram Central Railway Station

Cochin International Airport is the busiest Airport in Kerala by total passenger traffic

Kerala State Water Transport Department ferry at Ashtamudi Lake in Kollam, disembarking passengers

Roads

Kerala has 145,704 kilometres (90,536 mi) of roads, which accounts for 4.2% of India's total. This translates to about 4.62 kilometres (2.87 mi) of road per thousand population, compared to an average of 2.59 kilometres (1.61 mi) in the country. Roads in Kerala include 1,524 kilometres (947 mi) of national highway; 2.6% of the nation's total, 4,341.6 kilometres (2,697.7 mi) of state highway and 18,900 kilometres (11,700 mi) of district roads. Most of Kerala's west coast is accessible through the NH 66 (old NH 17 and 47); and the eastern side is accessible through state highways. New project for hill and coastal highways are announced now under KIIFB. National Highway 66, with the longest stretch of road (1,622 kilometres (1,008 mi)) connects Kanyakumari to Mumbai; it enters Kerala via Talapady in Kasargodand passes through Kannur, Kozhikode, Malappuram, Guruvayur, Kochi, Alappuzha, Kollam, Thiruvananthapuram before entering Tamil Nadu. Palakkad district is generally referred to as the Gateway of Kerala, due to the presence of the Palakkad Gap, in the Western Ghats, through which the northern (Malabar) and southern (Travancore) parts of Kerala are connected to the rest of India via road and rail. There is the state's largest checkpoint, Walayar, in NH 544, the border town between Kerala and Tamil Nadu, through which a large amount of public and commercial transportation reaches the northern and central districts of Kerala.

The Department of Public Works is responsible for maintaining and expanding the state highways system and major district roads. The Kerala State Transport Project (KSTP), which includes the GIS-based Road Information and Management Project (RIMS), is responsible for maintaining and expanding the state highways in Kerala; it also oversees a few major district roads. Traffic in Kerala has been growing at a rate of 10–11% every year, resulting in high traffic and pressure on the roads. Traffic density is nearly four times the national average, reflecting the state's high population. Kerala's annual total of road accidents is among the nation's highest. The accidents are mainly the result of the narrow roads and irresponsible driving. National Highways in Kerala are among the narrowest in the country and will remain so for the foreseeable future, as the state government has received an exemption that allows narrow national highways. In Kerala, highways are 45 metres (148 feet) wide. In other states National Highways are grade separated highways 60 metres (200 feet) wide with a minimum of four lanes, as well as 6 or 8 lane access-controlled expressways. National Highways Authority of India (NHAI) has threatened the Kerala state government that it will give high priority to other states in highway development as political commitment to better highways has been lacking. As of 2013, the state had the highest road accident rate in the country, with most fatal accidents taking place along the state's National Highways.

Railways

Kochi Metro train at PalarivattomMetro station

The Indian Railways' Southern Railway line runs through the state connecting most of the major towns and cities except those in the highland districts of Idukki and Wayanad. The railway network in the state is controlled by two out of six divisions of the Southern Railway; Thiruvananthapuram Railway division and Palakkad Railway Division. Thiruvananthapuram Central (TVC) is the largest railway station in the state. Kerala's major railway stations are:

- Thiruvananthapuram Central (TVC)
- Ernakulam Junction (South) (ERS)
- Kozhikode (CLT)
- Kollam Junction (QLN)
- Thrissur (TCR)
- Palakkad Junction (PGT)
- Kannur (CAN)
- Shornur Junction (SRR)
- Ernakulam Town (North) (ERN)
- Kottayam (KTYM)
- Chengannur (CNGR)
- Alappuzha (ALLP)
- Kochuveli Railway Station (KCVL)
- Kayamkulam Junction (KYJ)
- Tirur (TIR)
- Kasaragod (KGQ)
- Aluva (AWY)

Major railway transport between Beypore–Tirur began on 12 March 1861, from Shoranur–Cochin Harbour section in 1902, from Kollam–Sengottai on 1 July 1904, Kollam–Thiruvananthapuram on 4 January 1918, from Nilambur-Shoranur in 1927, from Ernakulam–Kottayam in 1956, from Kottayam–Kollam in 1958, from Thiruvananthapuram–Kanyakumari in 1979 and from the Thrissur-Guruvayur Section in 1994.

Kochi Metro is the metro system for the city of Kochi. It is the only metro in Kerala. The construction began in 2012 and the first phase set up at an estimated cost of 5181 crore (US$770 million).

Airports

Kerala has three international airports: Trivandrum International Airport, Cochin International Airport and Calicut International Airport. All civilian airports operating in the state are international ones, a feature which is unique to Kerala, which is the only state in India without a purely domestic airport. Construction of Kannur International Airport is completed and the airport is scheduled to open by the end of 2018.

Kollam Airport, established under the Madras Presidency and closed before the inauguration of Trivandrum International Airport in the capital, was the first airport in Kerala.

Trivandrum International Airport, managed by the Airport Authority of India, is among the oldest existing airports in South India.

Cochin International Airport is the busiest in the state and the seventh-busiest in the country. It was the first Indian airport to be incorporated as a public limited company; it was funded by nearly 10,000 non-resident Indiansfrom 30 countries. Cochin Airport is the primary hub of Air India Express and the secondary hub of Air Asia India.

Other than civilian airports, Kochi has a naval airport named INS Garuda. Thiruvananthapuram airport shares civilian facilities with the Southern Air Command of the Indian Air Force. These facilities are used mostly by central government VIPs visiting Kerala.

Water transport

Kerala has one major port, 17 minor ports and a few mini ports. The state has numerous backwaters, which are used for commercial inland navigation. Transport services are mainly provided by country craft and passenger vessels. There are 67 navigable rivers in the state while the total length of inland waterways is 1,687 kilometres (1,048 mi).

Port of Quilon: A distant view

The main constraints to the expansion of inland navigation are; lack of depth in waterways caused by silting, lack of maintenance of navigation systems and bank protection, accelerated growth of the water hyacinth, lack of modern inland craft terminals, and lack of a cargo handling system. A canal 205 kilometres (127 mi) long, National Waterway 3, runs between Kottapuram and Kollam, which is included in the East-Coast Canal.

AGRICULTURE AND LIVESTOCK

Kerala produces 97% of national output of pepper and accounts for 85% of the area under natural rubber in the country.Coconut, tea, coffee, cashew, and spices — including cardamom, vanilla, cinnamon, and nutmeg — comprise a critical agricultural sector. A key agricultural staple is rice, with some six hundred varieties grown in Kerala's extensive paddy fields.Nevertheless, home gardens comprise a significant portion of the agricultural sector. Related animal husbandry is also important, and is touted by proponents as a means of alleviating rural poverty and unemployment among women, the marginalised, and the landless. Feeding, milking, breeding, management, health care, and concomitant micro-enterprises all provide work for around 3.2 million of Kerala's 5.5 million households. The state government seeks to promote such activity via educational campaigns and the development of new cattle breeds such as Sunandini.

Given below is a table of 2015 national output share of select agricultural crops and allied segments in Kerala based on 2011 prices

Segment	National Share %
Palmyra	100.0
Nutmeg	99.8
Clove	95.6
Rubber	84.1
Cardamom	70.2
Pepper	64.8
Tapioca	48.3
Coconut	35.8
Tamarind	27.4
Jackfruit	18.8
Arecanut	16.9
Cocoa	15.5
Pineapple	12.7
Condiments and spices	9.7
Marine fish	8.3
Fuel wood	5.3
Banana	5.2
Coffee	5.2
Meat	5.1

The most essential or the staple crop is the rice or paddy. About 600 varieties of rice are grown in the sprawling paddy fields of Kerala. In fact the Kuttanad region of the district of Kerala is known as the 'rice bowl of the state' and enjoys a significant status in the production of rice.

Next to rice is Tapioca and is cultivated mainly in the drier regions. Tapioca is a major food of the Keralites. Besides production of the main crop, Kerala is also a major producer of spices that form the cash crops of the state. The important spices are cardamom, cinnamon, clove, turmeric, nutmeg and vanilla.

Other cash crops that constitute the agricultural sector include tea, coffee cashew, pulses, areca nut, ginger and coconut. In fact coconut provides the principal source of income in Kerala- from coir industry to coconut shell artifacts. Cashew is also an essential cash crop. Kottayam district has extensive areas producing and processing rubber. Apart from rubber, other plantation crop likes plantains or bananas are also grown in plenty.

National Sample Survey Organization (NSSO) conducted a Situation Assessment Survey in 2013. According to their data, as opposed to 57.8% of national households declaring themselves as agricultural, 27.3% did so in Kerala. And of those households in Kerala, nearly two-thirds earn income from activities other than agriculture.When statistics sum up the state earns 30 percent of its income from agriculture.

In 1960-61, Kerala contributed to nearly 70% of the country's coconut production. In 2011-12, it was at 42%. It dropped further by 2.3% points the next year. According to the State Planning Board (2011) data, the state is producing only about 12% of its total requirement for rice. In 1960-61 Kerala produced more than 10 lakh tons of rice. By 2012-13 rice production was down to 5.08 lakh tons. By 2012-13, in just a single year, area under rice cultivation had declined by 5.2%, and the production itself dropped by 10.2%.

Alcohol

The government enforces state monopoly over liquor sale in the state, after the state banned foreign liquor shops, through the government owned Kerala State Beverages Corporation (KSBC). Every year, liquor sales have been rising and the total sales of liquor and beer during 2010-11 fiscal year was expected to be about Rs. 67 billion.

The government applies the highest state tax on liquor (around 120%). The total revenue from taxes on liquor was Rs. 55.39 billion in 2009-10. Rum and brandy are the preferred drinks in Kerala in a country where whisky outsells every other liquor. Taxes on alcohol was a major source of revenue for the state government, but of late, it has been showing a declining trend. Only 4.2% of revenues for its annual budget come from liquor sales. Revenues from alcohol to the state's exchequer have registered a 100% rise over the past four years.

Liquor sales stood at 201 lakh cases worth Rs.11,577 crore during 2015-16, down from 220 lakh cases worth Rs.10,013 crore during the previous year. Gross sales during the first three months of 2016 were around Rs.4,000 crore.

Numbers from the Kerala State Beverages Corporation analyzed by the Alcohol and Drug Information Center (AIDIC), show that alcohol consumption dropped by 20.27 per cent since April 2014, this in a market that registered an annual growth of 12 per cent to 67 per cent for the last 30 years.

Chemical industry

Aluva is the largest industrial belt in Kerala. There are more than 247 industries viz. Fertilisers and Chemicals Travancore (FACT), Travancore Cochin Chemicals, Indian Rare Earths Limited, Hindustan Insecticides Limited and many others manufacturing a range of products like chemical-petrochemicalproducts, pesticides, rare-earth elements, rubber processing chemicals, fertilizers, zinc/chromium compounds and leather products.

Tourism

Kerala is an established tourist destination for both Indians and non-Indians alike. Tourism contributes to nearly 10% of the state's GDP. Tourists mostly visit, varkala, kovalam, fort kochi, Kappad, the hill stations of Munnar, Nelliampathi, Wayanad and Ponmudi, and national parks and wildlife sanctuaries such as Periyar and Eravikulam National Park. The "backwaters" region – an extensive network of interlocking rivers, lakes, and canals that center on Veli, Akkulam, Ashtamudi, Alleppey,

Kumarakom, and Punnamada – also see heavy tourist traffic. Examples of Keralite architecture, such as the Padmanabhapuram Palace, Malik Deenar Mosque Kasaragod, Paradesi Synagogue are also visited. cities like Kozhikode (Land of Zamorins) and Alappuzha(called the "Venice of the East") are also popular destinations.

A house Boat View from Vembanad Lake

Tourism plays an important role in the state's economy. Kerala is also a preferred destination for night dwellers and the nightlife districts in Kochi, Kozhikode, Thrissur, Kottayam and Kollam are the major centres. Along with tourism there is also a new trend of domestic pilgrimage tourism visible in Kerala in recent years during the annual Sabarimala pilgrimage season and round the year to temples such as Padmanabhaswamy Temple Thiruvananthapuram, Guruvayur Temple Thrissur etc.

BSE listed Kerala companies

1. Geojit Financial Services
2. V-Guard Industries Ltd
3. Federal Bank
4. Dhanlaxmi Bank
5. South Indian Bank
6. Cochin Minerals and Rutile Limited
7. Manappuram Finance Limited
8. Muthoot Finance
9. Harrisons Malayalam
10. Accel Transmatic Limited
11. GTN Textiles Limited
12. Kitex Garments
13. Nitta Gelatin India Ltd
14. Eastern Treads Limited
15. Rubfila International LTD
16. Kerala Ayurveda Ltd
17. Vertex Securities Ltd
18. Sree Sakthi Paper Mills
19. AVT Natural Products
20. Victory Paper and Boards (India) Limited
21. Cochin Shipyard Limited
22. Aster DM Healthcare Limited

Foreign remittances

In a state of 32 million where unemployment approaches 20 percent, one out of six employed Keralite now works overseas.

As of 2008, the Gulf countries altogether have a Keralite population of more than 2.5 million, who send home annually a sum of USD 9.25 billion, which is more than 15.13% of Remittance to India in 2008. Large numbers work in construction. High literacy allows Keralites to secure administrative employment & white collar jobs. Foreign remittances augment the state's economic output by nearly 25 percent. Migrants' families are three times as likely as those of nonmigrants to live in superior housing, and about twice as likely to have telephones, refrigerators and cars. Pathanamthittaand Thrissur districts have on an average one member from each household a non-resident Indian.

Of the $71 billion in remittances sent to India in 2012, Kerala still received the highest among the states: $11.3 billion, which is nearly 16%.

The survey conducted by the Centre for Development Studies (CDS), Thiruvananthapuram, in 2016 pointed out that foreign remittances in Kerala in 2014 was estimated to be Rs. 71,142 crores which dropped to Rs.63,289 crores in 2016. It is estimated that the state received annual remittances in 2017, amounting to Rs 90,000 crore, which is 35% of the state's income.

According to a study commissioned by the Kerala State Planning Board, the state should look for other reliable sources instead of relying on remittances to finance its expenditure.

Banking

Kerala is the single largest originator of education loans for the country as a whole.Total disbursal of education loans amount to Rs. 60 billion.

Ship building

The Cochin Shipyard in Kochi is the largest ship building facility in India. Cochin Shipyard was incorporated in the year 1972 as a fully owned Government of India company. In the last three decades the company has emerged as a forerunner in the Indian shipbuilding & Shiprepair industry. This yard can build and repair the largest vessels in India. It can build ships up to 1,100,000 tonnes deadweight (DWT) and repair ships up to

1,250,000 DWT. The yard has delivered two of India's largest double hull Aframax tankers each of 95,000 DWT. CSL has secured shipbuilding orders from internationally renowned companies from Europe & Middle East and is nominated to build the country's first indigenously built Air Defence Ship. The Cochin Shipyard also builds ships for the Indian Navy.

Shipyard commenced ship repair operations in the year 1982 and has undertaken repairs of all types of ships including upgradation of ships of oil exploration industry as well as periodical lay up repairs and life extension of ships of Navy, UTL, Coast Guard, Fisheries and Port Trust besides merchant ships of SCI & ONGC. The yard has, over the years, developed adequate capabilities to handle complex and sophisticated repair jobs. Recently Cochin Shipyard won a major repair orders from ONGC. The order for major repairs of three rigs viz Mobile Offshore Drilling Unit (MODU) Sagar Vijay, Mobile Offshore Drilling Unit (MODU) Sagar Bhushan and Jack Up Rig (JUR) Sagar Kiran was secured by CSL against very stiff international competition.

Oil Refining and Petrochemicals

The Kochi Refinery is a public crude oil refinery in the city of Kochi. It is the largest state owned refinery in India with a production capacity of 15.5 million tons per annum.Formerly known as Cochin Refineries Limited and later renamed as Kochi Refineries Limited, it was acquired by Bharat Petroleum Corporation Limited in the year 2006. Today Kochi Refinery is a frontline entity as the unit of the Fortune 500 company, BPCL. With a turnover of around US$2500 million, the refinery aims to strengthen its presence in refining and marketing of petroleum products and further grow into the energy and petrochemical sectors.

Kochi Refinery is engaged in Refining and marketing of petroleum products. Beginning with a capacity of 50,000 barrels per day (7,900 m3/d)(bpd), today the Refinery has a refining capacity of 190,000 bbl/d (30,000 m3/d). The Company entered the petrochemical sector with benzene and toluene in 1989.

INFRASTRUCTURE

Kerala has 145,704 km of roads (4.2% of India's total). This translates into about 4.62 km of road per thousand population, compared to an all-India average of 2.59 km. Virtually all of Kerala's villages are connected by road. Traffic in Kerala has been growing at a rate of 10–11% every year, resulting in high traffic and pressure on the roads. Total road length in Kerala increased by 5% between 2003-2004. The road density in Kerala is nearly four times the national average, and is a reflection of Kerala's unique settlement patterns. India's national highway network includes a Kerala-wide total of 1,524 km, which is only 2.6% of the national total. There are eight designated national highways in the state. Upgrading and maintenance of 1,600 km of state highways and major district roads have been taken up under the Kerala State Transport Project (KSTP), which includes the GIS-based Road Information and Management Project (RIMS). Kerala ranks second nationwide in diesel-based thermal electricity generation with national market share of over 21%.

Energy

India's largest floating solar power plant set up on the Banasura Sagar reservoir in Wayanad, Kerala. It is the 500 kWp (kilowatt peak) solar plant of the Kerala state electricity board (KSEB) floats on 1.25 acres of water surface of the reservoir.

7

Tourism

INTRODUCTION

Kerala, a state situated on the tropical Malabar Coast of southwestern India, is one of the most popular tourist destinations in the country. Named as one of the *ten paradises of the world* by *National Geographic Traveler*, Kerala is famous especially for its ecotourism initiatives and beautiful backwaters. Its unique culture and traditions, coupled with its varied demography, have made Kerala one of the most popular tourist destinations in the world. Growing at a rate of 13.31%, the tourism industry is a major contributor to the state's economy.

Kerala's culture and traditions, coupled with its varied demographics, have made the state one of the most popular tourist destinations in India. In 2012, National Geographic's Traveller magazine named Kerala as one of the "ten paradises of the world" and "50 must see destinations of a lifetime". Travel and Leisure also described Kerala as "One of the 100 great trips for the 21st century". In 2012, it overtook the Taj Mahal to be the number one travel destination in Google's search trends for India. Kerala's beaches, backwaters, lakes, mountain ranges, waterfalls, ancient ports, palaces, religious institutions and wildlife sanctuaries are major attractions for both domestic and international tourists. The city of Kochi ranks first in the total number of international and domestic tourists in Kerala. Until the early 1980s, Kerala was a relatively unknown destination compared to other states in the country. In 1986 the government of Kerala declared tourism an important industry and it was the first state in India to do so.Marketing campaigns launched by the Kerala Tourism Development Corporation, the government agency that oversees the tourism prospects of the state, resulted in the growth of the tourism industry. Many advertisements branded Kerala with the tagline *Kerala, God's Own Country*. Kerala tourism is a global brand and regarded as one of the destinations with highest recall. In 2006, Kerala attracted 8.5 million tourists, an increase of 23.68% over the previous year, making the state one of the fastest-growing popular destinations in the world. In 2011, tourist inflow to Kerala crossed the 10-million mark.

Ayurvedic tourism has become very popular since the 1990s, and private agencies have played a notable role in tandem with the initiatives of the Tourism Department. Kerala is known for its ecotourism initiatives which include mountaineering, trekking and bird-watching programmes in the Western Ghats as the major activities. As of 2005, the state's tourism industry was a major contributor to the state's economy, growing at the rate of 13.31%. The revenue from tourism increased five-fold between 2001 and 2011 and crossed the 190 billion mark in 2011. Moreover, the industry provides employment to approximately 1.2 million people.

Asia's largest, and the world's third-largest, Naval Academy-Ezhimala Naval Academy-at Kannur is in Kerala. The state's only drive-in beach, Muzhappilangad in Kannur, which stretches across four kilometres of sand, was chosen by the BBC as one of the top six drive-in beaches in the world in 2016. Idukki arch dam, the world's second arch dam, and Asia's first, is in Kerala. The major beaches are at Kovalam, Varkala, Fort Kochi, Cherai, Alappuzha, Payyambalam, Kappad, Muzhappilangad (South India's only drive-in beach) and Bekal. Popular hill stations are at Wayanad, Wagamon, Munnar, Peermade, Paithalmala of Kannur district, Nelliampathi and Ponmudi. Munnar is 4,500 feet above sea level and is known for tea plantations, and a variety of flora and fauna. Kerala's ecotourism destinations include 12 wildlife sanctuaries and two national parks: Periyar Tiger Reserve, Parambikulam Wildlife Sanctuary, Chinnar

Wildlife Sanctuary, Thattekad Bird Sanctuary, Wayanad Wildlife Sanctuary, Muthanga Wildlife Sanctuary, Aralam Wildlife Sanctuary, Eravikulam National Park, and Silent Valley National Park are the most popular among them. The Kerala backwaters are an extensive network of interlocking rivers (41 west-flowing rivers), lakes, and canals that centre around Alleppey, Kumarakom and Punnamada (where the annual Nehru Trophy Boat Race is held in August), Pathiramanal a small island in Muhamma . Padmanabhapuram Palace and the Mattancherry Palace are two nearby heritage sites.

An evening view of Kollam Beach

Until the early 1980s, Kerala was a relatively unknown destination, with most tourism circuits concentrated around the north of the country. Aggressive marketing campaigns launched by the Kerala Tourism Development Corporation—the government agency that oversees tourism prospects of the state—laid the foundation for the growth of the tourism industry. In the decades that followed, Kerala Tourism was able to transform itself into one of the niche holiday destinations in India. The tag line *Kerala – God's Own Country* was adopted in its tourism promotions and became a global superbrand. Kerala is regarded as one of the destinations with the highest brand recall. In 2010, Kerala attracted 660,000 foreign tourist arrivals.

Kerala is an established destination for both domestic as well as foreign tourists. Kerala is well known for its beaches, backwaters in Alappuzha and Kollam, mountain ranges and wildlife sanctuaries. Other popular attractions in the state include the beaches at Kovalam, Varkala, Kollam and Kapad; backwater tourism and lake resorts around Ashtamudi Lake, Kollam; hill stations and resorts at Munnar, Wayanad, Nelliampathi, Vagamon and Ponmudi; and national parks and wildlife sanctuaries at Periyar, Parambikulam and Eravikulam National Park. The "backwaters" region—an extensive network of interlocking rivers, lakes, and canals that centre on Ashtamudi Lake, Kollam, also see heavy tourist traffic. Heritage sites, such as the Padmanabhapuram Palace, Hill Palace, and Mattancherry Palace, are also visited. The city of Kochi ranks first in the total number of international and domestic tourists in Kerala. To further promote tourism in Kerala, the Grand Kerala Shopping Festival was started by the Government of Kerala in 2007. Since then it has been held every year during the December–January period.

The state's tourism agenda promotes ecologically sustained tourism, which focuses on the local culture, wilderness adventures, volunteering and personal growth of the local population. Efforts are taken to minimise the adverse effects of traditional tourism on the natural environment, and enhance the cultural integrity of local people.

Historical context

Since its incorporation as a state, Kerala's economy largely operated under welfare-based democratic socialist principles. This mode of development, though it resulted in a high Human Development Index and standard of living among the people, led to an economic stagnationin the 1980s (growth rate of 2.3% annually).) This apparent paradox—high human development and low economic development—led to a large number of educated unemployed seeking jobs overseas, especially in the Gulf countries.

Due to the large number of expatriates, many travel operators and agencies set up shop in the state to facilitate their travel needs. However, the trends soon reciprocated, with the travel agencies noticing the undermined potential of the state as a tourist destination. The first travel agency in Kerala, Kerala Travels, was founded by Col G.V. Raja of the Travancore royal family along with P.G.C. Pillai.

By 1986, tourism had gained an industry status. Kerala Tourism subsequently adopted the tagline *God's Own Country* in its advertisement campaigns. Aggressive promotion in print and electronic media were able to invite a sizable investment in the hospitality industry. By the early 2000s, tourism had grown into a full–fledged, multibillion-dollar industry in the state. The state was able to carve a niche for itself in the world tourism industry, thus becoming one of the places with the "highest brand recall". In 2003, Kerala, a hitherto unknown tourism destination, became the fastest growing tourism destination in the world. Today, growing at a rate of 13.31%, Kerala is one of the most visited tourism destinations in India.

Major attractions

Varkala Beach, Trivandrum

Beaches

Flanked on the western coast by the Arabian Sea, Kerala has a long coastline of 580 km (360 mi); all of which is virtually dotted with sandy beaches.

Boating at Paravur Lake near Kollam

Kovalam beach near Thiruvananthapuram was among the first beaches in Kerala to attract tourists. Rediscovered by back-packers and tan-seekers in the 1960s and followed by hordes of hippies in the 1970s, Kovalam is today the most visited beach in the state.

Other popularly visited beaches in the state include those at Kappad, Alappuzha, Marari Beach(Mararikulam, Alappuzha), Nattika (Thrissur), Vadanappilly beach (Thrissur), Cherai Beach, Beypore beach, Marari beach, Fort Kochi, and Varkala. The Muzhappilangad Beachat Kannur is the only drive-in beach in India. Marari beach was rated as one of the worlds top five HAMMOCK BEACH by National Geographic survey. Payambalam beach is one of the most beautiful beach in Kerala situated in Kannur. Other beaches in Kannur include baby beach, meenkunnu beach, azhikode beach, madaiparra beach, chootath beach, mermaid beach.

Backwaters

The backwaters in Kerala are a chain of brackish lagoons

and lakes lying parallel to the Arabian Sea coast (known as the Malabar Coast). *Houseboat* or *Kettuvallam* rides in the backwaters are a major tourist attraction. Backwater tourism is centered mostly around Ashtamudi Lake, Kollam. Boat races held during festival seasons are also a major tourist attraction in the backwater regions.

The backwater network includes large lakes such as the Ashtamudi Lake, the largest among them, linked by 1500 km of canals, both man-made and natural and fed by several rivers, and extending virtually the entire length of Kerala state. The backwaters were formed by the action of waves and shore currents creating low barrier islands across the mouths of the many rivers flowing down from the Western Ghats range.

Backwaters in Kerala for honeymoon and family holiday are quite popular. You may short some best Kerala backwaters tour packages after reading about Kerala backwaters reviews available on various websites.

Hill stations

Munnar Hillscape

Eastern Kerala consists of land encroached upon by the Western Ghats; the region thus includes high mountains, gorges, and deep-cut valleys. The wildest lands are covered with dense forests, while other regions lie under tea and coffee plantations (established mainly in the 19th and 20th centuries) or other forms of cultivation.

The Western Ghats rise on average to 1500 m elevation above sea level. Some of the popular hill stations in the region are Munnar, Vagamon, Paithalmala, Wayanad, Nelliyampathi, Elapeedika, Peermade, Thekkady and Ponmudi.

Wildlife

The Konni Elephant Training Centre near Pathanamthitta

Most of Kerala, whose native habitat consists of wet evergreen rainforests at lower elevations and highland deciduous and semi-evergreen forests in the east, is subject to a humid tropical climate. However, significant variations in terrain and elevation have resulted in a land whose biodiversityregisters as among the world's most significant. Most of Kerala's significantly biodiverse tracts of wilderness lie in the evergreen forests of its easternmost districts. Kerala also hosts two of the world's Ramsar Convention-listed wetlands: Lake Sasthamkotta and the Vembanad-Kol wetlands are noted as being wetlands of international importance.

There are also numerous protected conservation areas, including 1455.4 km^2 of the vast Nilgiri Biosphere Reserve. In turn, the forests play host to such major fauna as Asian elephant (*Elephas maximus*), Bengal tiger (*Panthera tigris tigris*), leopard (*Panthera pardus*), Nilgiri tahr (*Nilgiritragus hylocrius*), and grizzled giant squirrel (*Ratufa macroura*).

More remote preserves, including Silent Valley National Park in the Kundali Hills, harbour endangered species such as the lion-tailed macaque (*Macaca silenus*), Indian sloth bear (*Melursus (Ursus) ursinus ursinus*), and gaur (the so-called "Indian bison"—*Bos gaurus*).

More common species include Indian porcupine (*Hystrix indica*), chital (*Axis axis*), sambar (*Cervus unicolor*), gray langur, flying squirrel, swamp lynx (*Felis chaus kutas*), boar (*Sus scrofa*), a variety of catarrhine Old World monkey species, gray wolf (*Canis lupus*), and common palm civet (*Paradoxurus hermaphroditus*). Many reptiles, such as king cobra, viper, python, various turtles and crocodiles are to be found in Kerala—again, disproportionately in the east.

Kerala's avifauna include endemics like the Sri Lanka frogmouth(*Batrachostomus moniliger*), Oriental bay owl, large frugivores like the great hornbill (*Buceros bicornis*) and Indian grey hornbill, as well as the more widespread birds such as peafowl, Indian cormorant, jungle and hill myna, Oriental darter, black-hooded oriole, greater racket-tailed and black drongoes, bulbul (*Pycnonotidae*), species of kingfisher and woodpecker, jungle fowl, Alexandrine parakeet, and assorted ducks and migratory birds. Additionally, freshwater fish such as *kadu* (stinging catfish—*Heteropneustes* fossilis) and brackishwater species such as *Choottachi* (orange chromide—*Etroplus maculatus*, valued as an aquarium specimen) also are native to Kerala's lakes and waterways.

Waterfalls

Meenvallam falls

- Adyanpara Falls, near Nilambur
- Aruvikkuzhi, near Maramon, Kozhencherry in Pathanamthitta District
- Aruvikkuzhi, near Pallickathode, Kottayam District
- Athirappilly Falls 80 ft (24 m)
- Charpa Falls
- Cheeyappara Falls, near Adimali
- Chethalayam Falls, in Wayanad
- Kumbhavurutty Falls in Kollam district
- Lakkom Water Falls

- Madatharuvi Falls, near Ranny in Pathanamthitta District
- Marmala waterfall
- Meenmutty Falls, Thiruvananthapuram
- Meenmutty Falls 984 ft (300 m), in Wayanad
- Mulamkuzhi, near Malayattoor in Ernakulam District
- Panieli Poru waterfalls Ernakulam
- Palaruvi Falls, 300 ft (91 m) in Aryankavu near Punalur in Kollam district
- Pattathippara Falls
- Perunthenaruvi Falls
- Siruvani Waterfalls Palakkad
- Soochipara Falls 656 ft (200 m) / Sentinelrock falls, in Wayanad
- Thommankuthu Falls, near Thodupuzha
- Thusharagiri Falls
- Valara Falls, near Adimali
- Vazhachal Falls, near Athirappilly
- Vazhvanthol waterfalls Trivandrum

Lighthouses

Lighthouses are the main centre of attractions of Kerala beaches and coast line. There are 15 lighthouses in the entire state of Kerala. Districts of Kollam, Kannur, Kozhikode, Alappuzha, Thrissur and Thiruvananthapuram have more than one lighthouse.

Major Lighthouses

- Vizhinjam lighthouse, Thiruvananthapuram
- Anjengo lighthouse, Thiruvananthapuram
- Tangasseri Lighthouse, Kollam
- Kovilthottam Lighthouse, Kollam
- Alappuzha Lighthouse, Alappuzha
- Manakkodam Lighthouse, Alappuzha

- Cochin Lighthouse, Ernakulam(*Tallest in the state*)
- Azhikode Lighthouse, Thrissur
- Chetwai Lighthouse, Thrissur
- Ponnani Lighthouse, Malappuram
- Beypore Lighthouse, Kozhikode
- Kozhikode lighthouse, Kozhikode (Defunct)
- Cannanore Lighthouse, Kannur
- Mount Dilly Lighthouse, Kannur
- Kasargode Lighthouse, Kasargode

Events

Festivals

Thirayattam (kuttychathan) An Ethnic Ritual Performing Art Form In Kerala State, India.

The major festival in Kerala is Onam. Kerala has a number of religious festivals. Thrissur Pooram, Attukal Pongala, Beema Palli Uroos, and Chettikulangara Bharani are the major temple festivals in Kerala. The Thrissur Pooram is conducted at the Vadakumnathan temple, Thrissur.

Panchavadyam

Shashti

The Chettikulangara Bharani is another major attraction. The festival is conducted at the Chettikulangara temple near Mavelikkara. The Sivarathri is also an important festival in Kerala. This festival is mainly celebrated in Aluva Temple and Padanilam Parabrahma Temple. Padanilam Temple is situated in Alappuzha district of Kerala, about 16 kilometres (9.9 mi) from Mavelikkara town. *Parumala Perunnal, Manarkadu Perunnal* are the major festivals of Christians. Muslims also have many important festivals. Annual festival Thirayattam is conducted Sacred groves and village shrine of south malabar region (kozhikode and malappuram districts) in Kerala. "Thirayattam" is a vibrant Ethnic performing art. it is an admixture of dance,drama, songs,instrumental music,facial and body makeup, satire, martial art and ritualistic function, composed in a harmonizing manner.

Kochi-Muziris Biennale

Kerala is also known for the many events conducted by the Ministry of Tourism for tourist attractions. Kochi-Muziris

Biennale, the first Biennale in India was conducted in Kochi from 12 December 2012 till 13 March 2013.The government contributed about 12-150 million on the event. An International Coir Fest is conducted annually that is aimed at developing the coir industry of Kerala and tourism.

Grand Kerala Shopping Festival

To further promote tourism in Kerala, the Government of Kerala started the Grand Kerala Shopping Festival in the year 2007. Since then it has become an annual shopping event being conducted in the December–January period.

During this period stores and shops registered under the GKSF offer a wide range of discounts, VAT refunds, etc. Along with the guaranteed shopping experience, shoppers are provided with gift coupons for a fixed worth of purchase entering them into weekly and mega lucky draws.

As compared to shopping festivals held in other countries, this Festival converts the entire state of Kerala into a giant shopping mall, incorporating not just the big players, but also the small and medium scale industries. Through this shopping festival, the Kerala Government intends to transform the State into a hub for international shopping experience and thereby launch “Shopping Tourism” in the state.

Ayurveda

Medical tourism, promoted by traditional systems of medicine like Ayurveda and Siddha, is widely popular in the state, and draws increasing numbers of tourists. A combination of many factors has led to the increase in popularity of medical tourism: high costs of healthcare in industrialised nations, ease and affordability of international travel, improving technology and standards of care.

However, rampant recent growth in this sector has made the government apprehensive. The government is now considering introduction of a grading system which would grade hospitals and clinics, thus helping tourists in selecting one for their treatments.

Culture

Kerala's culture is mainly Hindu in origin, deriving from a greater Tamil-heritage region known as Tamilakam. Later, Kerala's culture was elaborated on through centuries of contact with overseas cultures. Native performing arts include *koodiyattom*, *kathakali*—from *katha* ("story") and *kali*("play")—and its offshoot *Kerala Natanam*, *koothu* (akin to stand-up comedy), *mohiniaattam*("dance of the enchantress"), *thullal*, *padayani*, *thirayattam*, and *theyyam*. Other arts are more religion- and tribal-themed. These include *chavittu nadakom*, *oppana* (originally from Malabar), which combines dance, rhythmic hand clapping, and *ishal* vocalisations. However, many of these art forms largely play to tourists or at youth festivals, and are not as popular among most ordinary Keralites, who look to more contemporary art and performance styles, including those employing mimicry and parody. Additionally, a substantial Malayalam film industry effectively competes against both Bollywood and Hollywood.

Several ancient ritualised arts are Keralite in origin; these include *kalaripayattu* (*kalari* ("place", "threshing floor", or "battlefield") and *payattu* ("exercise" or "practice")). Among the world's oldest martial arts, oral tradition attributes *kalaripayattu*'s emergence to Parasurama. Other ritual arts include*Thirayattam*, *theyyam*, *poorakkali* and *Kuthiyottam*. Thirayattam is a ritual performing folk aet form of south malabe region in kerala.This vibrant art form blend of dance, music, theatre, satire, facial & body painting, masking, martial art and ritualistic function.Thirayattam enacted i courtyards of "Kaavukal"(sacred groves)and village shrine.

Kuthiyottam is a ritualistic symbolic representation of human bali (homicide). Folklore exponents see this art form, with enchanting well–structured choreography and songs, as one among the rare Adi Dravida folklore traditions still preserved and practised in Central Kerala in accordance with the true tradition and environment. Typical to the Adi Dravida folk dances and songs, the movements and formations of dancers (clad in white thorthu and banyan) choreographed in Kuthiyottam are quick, peaks at a particular point and ends abruptly. The traditional songs also start in a stylish slow pace, then gain momentum and end abruptly.

A procession of gold-caparisoned Kerala elephants at the Thrissur Pooram

Kuthiyotta Kalaris', run by Kuthiyotta Ashans (Teachers or leaders), train the group to perform the dances and songs. Normally, the training starts about one to two months before the season. Young boys between 8 and 14 years are taught Kuthiyottam, a ritual dance in the house amidst a big social gathering before the portrait of the deity. Early in the morning on Bharani, after the feast and other rituals, the boys whose bodies are coiled with silver wires, one end of which is tied around his neck and an arecanut fixed on the tip of a knife held high over his head, are taken in procession to the temple with the accompaniment of beating of drums, music, ornamental umbrellas, and other classical folk art forms, and richly caparisoned elephants.

All through the way to the temple tender coconut water will be continually poured on his body. After the circumambulation the boys stands at a position facing the Sreekovil (Sanctum Sanctorum) and begins to dance. This ceremony ends with dragging the coil pierced to the skin whereby a few drops of blood comes out.

On this day just after midday the residents of the locality bring huge decorated effigies of Bhima panchalia, Hanuman and extremely beautiful tall chariots in wheeled platforms, and after having darshan the parties take up their respective position in the paddy fields lying east of the temple.

During the night, the image of Devi will be carried in procession to the effigies stationed in the paddy fields. On the next day these structures will be taken back. A big bazaar is also held at Chetikulangara as part of this festival. Kuthiyottam is the main vazipadu of the Chettikulangara temple, Mavelikkara.

In respect of Fine Arts, the State has an abounding tradition of both ancient and contemporary art and artists.The traditional Kerala murals are found in ancient temples, churches and palaces across the State. These paintings, mostly dating to between the 9th to 12th centuries AD, display a distinct style, and a colour code which is predominantly ochre and green.

Like the rest of India, religious diversity is very prominent in Kerala. The principal religions are Hinduism, Christianity, and Islam; Jainism, Judaism, Sikhism, and Buddhism have smaller followings. The state's historic ties with the rest of the world have resulted in the state having many famous temples, churches, and mosques notably 8 of the world's oldest churches—from the 1st century CE, founded by Thomas the Apostle when he reached Indian shores, the first mosque of India, which existed even before the death of the prophet Muhammad and the oldest active synagogue in the Commonwealth of Nations.

Recognising the potential of tourism in the diversity of religious faiths, related festivals and structures, the tourism department launched a "Pilgrimage tourism" project. Major pilgrim tourism attractions include Guruvayur, Sabarimala, Malayatoor, Paradesi Synagogue, St. Mary's Forane (Martha

Mariam) Church Kuravilangad built in 105 A.D, AttukalPongala (which has the Guinness record for being the largest gathering of women in the planet), and Chettikulangara Bharani.

Advertising campaigns

Kerala Tourism is noted for its innovative and market-focused ad campaigns. These campaigns have won the tourism department numerous awards, including the *Das Golden Stadttor Award for Best Commercial, 2006, Pacific Asia Travel Association- Gold Award for Marketing, 2003* and the Government of India's *Best Promotion Literature, 2004, Best Publishing, 2004* and *Best Tourism Film, 2001.*

Catchy slogans and innovative designs are considered a trademark of brand Kerala Tourism. Celebrity promotions are also used to attract more tourists to the state. The Kerala tourism website is widely visited, and has been the recipient of many awards. Recently, the tourism department has also engaged in advertising via mobiles, by setting up a WAPportal, and distributing wallpapers and ringtones related to Kerala through it.

Awards

The state has won numerous awards for its tourism initiatives. These include:

- 2016 - ITB-Berlin"s Golden City Gate Gold Award for Kerala tourism
- 2014 - ITB-Berlin's Golden City Gate Gold Award for Print Campaign
- 2014 -UNWTO Ulysses Award for Innovation in Public Policy and Governance for Sustainable Tourism
- 2012 - Kerala Tourism wins silver prize at the Golden Gate Award of the Internationale Tourismus-Börse Berlin
- 2005 - Nominated as one among the three finalists at the World Travel and Tourism Council's 'Tourism for Tomorrow' awards in the destination category
- Das Golden Stadttor Award for Best Commercial, 2006

Pacific Asia Travel Association

- Grand award for Environment, 2006
- Gold award for Ecotourism, 2006
- Gold award for Publication, 2006
- Gold Award for E-Newsletter, 2005
- Honourable Mention for Culture, 2005
- Gold Award for Culture, 2004
- Gold Award for Ecotourism, 2004
- Gold Award for CD-ROM, 2004 and 2003
- Gold Award for Marketing, 2003
- Grand Award for Heritage, 2002
- Pacific Asia Travel Writers Association
- International Award for Leisure Tourism, 2000–2001

Government of India

- Best Performing Tourism State, 2005
- Best Maintained Tourist-friendly Monument, 2005
- Best Publishing, 2005
- Best Marketed and Promoted State, 2004.
- Best Maintained Tourist-friendly Monument, 2004
- Best Innovative Tourism Project, 2004
- Best Promotion Literature, 2004
- Best Publishing, 2004
- Best Performing State for 2003, 2001, 2000 and 1999 - Award for Excellence in Tourism.
- Best Practices by a State Government, 2003
- Best Eco-tourism Product, 2003
- Best Wildlife Sanctuary, 2003
- Most Innovative Use of Information Technology, 2003 and 2001
- Most Tourist-friendly International Airport, 2002
- Most Eco-friendly Destination, 2002
- Best Tourism Film, 2001 (madivilikkunnu star in pavnlal)

Outlook Traveller - TAAI

- Best State that promoted Travel & Tourism, 2000–2001

Federation of Indian Chambers of Commerce and Industry

- Award for Best Marketing, 2003
- Award for Best Use of IT in Tourism, 2003

Galileo - Express Travel & Tourism

- Award for the Best Tourism Board, 2006
- Award for the Best State Tourism Board, 2003

Muziris Heritage Project

Muziris Heritage Project is a tourism venture by Tourism Department of Kerala to "reinstate the historical and cultural significance Muziris". The idea of the project came after the extensive excavations and discoveries at Pattanam by Kerala Council for Historical Research. The project also covers various other historically significant sites and monuments in central Kerala.

The nearby site of Kottapuram, a 16th-century fort, was also excavated (from May 2010) as part of the Muziris Heritage Project.

Department of Forests and Wildlife (Kerala)

Department of Forests and Wildlife (Kerala) : Headquarters and training centre are both located in Thiruvananthapuram city. More information on ecotourism destinations and permissions for trekking including arranging guides can be obtained through the department as well.

8

Population and Religion

KERALA POPULATION

Kerala is a state in India on the Malabar coast in the southwest region of the country. Kerala is bordered by Tamil Nadu to the south and east, Karnataka to the north and northeast, and the Lakshadweep Sea to the west.

Kerala has an estimated population of 35 million, up from 33.38 million in 2011. It is the 13th most populous state in India with an overall population density of 2,200 people per square mile, or 860 per square kilometer. Kerala is home to almost 3% of India's population and its land is three times more densely settled than the rest of the country.

The coastal regions are more populated than the mountains and eastern hills of the state with 2.5 times the overall population density.

Cities in Kerala

The capital of Kerala is Thirovananthapuram, which was called the "Evergreen city of India" by Mahatma Gandhi. The city has a population of 755,000 in the city proper but a population of 1.68 million in the urban agglomeration. This makes it the most populous city corporation and the fifth largest urban agglomeration in the state.

Other major cities in Kerala: Kochi (or Cochin) is a port city on the west coast with a population of 602,000 and a metropolitan population of 2.1 million. Kochi is the largest urban agglomeration in the state and the most densely populated city in Kerala with 16,400 people per square mile (6,340 per square kilometer). It is also considered a B-1 grade city by the Government of India, which makes it the highest graded city in the state.

Kannur (or Cannanore) is located about 518 kilometers north of the capital and it's the largest city in the North Malabar region and one of the oldest municipalities in Kerala. Kannur has a population of 64,000, with a metropolitan population of 1.64 million. Kozhikode (or Calicut) is the third-largest city in the state and part of the second-largest urban agglomeration in the state with a metropolitan population of 2.1 million. Kollam (or Quilon) is a sea port in Kerala and the 4th largest city in the state with a population of 350,000 and a metro population of 1.1 million.

Kerala Demographics

About 32 million Keralites are Malayali. 1.1% of the population (321,000) are indigenous tribal Adivasis and concentrated in the eastern part of the state. In 2013, there were nearly 2.5 million migrant workers from other states in Kerala, or 7.5% of the state's population.

Kerala has three main religions: Hinduism (56%), Islam (25%) and Christianity (19%). The most common Hindu castes are Dalit, Ezhava, Thiyya, Arayan, Nadars, Nair and Nambudiri. The most common Muslim organizations are Sunni, Mujahid and Jama'at-e-Islami. There was a large Jewish population in the region until the 1900s, when most moved to Israel.

Kerala has a Human Development Index of 0.79, which is "very high" and the highest in India. Kerala also has the highest literacy rates among all Indian states at 98.9%, and a life expectancy of 74 years which is among the highest in the country. Kerala has experienced a rapidly dropping rural poverty rate, which fell from 59% in the mid-1970s to 12% by 2010, while the overall poverty rate fell 47% between the 1970s and 2000s, compared to a drop of just 29% in overall poverty in the country.

Kerala has one of the lowest fertility rates in India, which has caused a demographics shift as seen in many developed countries with 12% of its population over the age of 60. Kerala is also considered the healthiest and cleanest state in India.

Kerala Population Growth

While Kerala has what appears to be rapid growth by the standards of most areas, its 4.9% decadal growth in 2011 was the lowest in India, and less than one third of the India average of 17.64%. Between 1951 and 1991, Kerala's population more than doubled from 15.6 million to 29.1 million, reaching 33.3 million by 2011.

Kerala is currently heading for zero growth in its population, as the state has a very low fertility rate and a stabilizing death rate. The zero growth rate is expected to happen within 25 years. In 2021, census figures predict Kerala will record negative population growth, which will be a first in India.

DEMOGRAPHICS

Languages of Kerala (2011)

Malayalam (97.03%)

Tamil (1.50%)

Others (1.47%)

Kerala is home to 2.76% of India's population; with a density of 859 persons per km^2, its land is nearly three times as densely settled as the Indian national average of 370 persons per km^2. As of 2011, Thiruvananthapuram is the most populous city in Kerala. In the state, the rate of population growth is India's lowest, and the decadal growth of 4.9% in 2011 is less than one third of the all-India average of 17.64%.Kerala's population more than doubled between 1951 and 1991 by adding 15.6 million people to reach 29.1 million residents in 1991; the population stood at 33.3 million by 2011. Kerala's coastal regions are the most densely settled with population of 2022 persons per km^2, 2.5 times the overall population density of the state, 859 persons per km^2, leaving the eastern hills and mountains comparatively sparsely populated. Around 31.8 million Keralites are predominantly Malayali. The state's 321,000 indigenous tribal

Adivasis, 1.10% of the population, are concentrated in the east. Malayalam, one of the classical languages in India, is Kerala's official language. Over a dozen other scheduled and unscheduled languages are also spoken. As of early 2013, there are close to 2.5 million (7.5% of the state population) migrant labourers in Kerala from other parts of India.

Gender

There is the tradition of matrilineal inheritance in Kerala, where the mother is the head of the household. As a result, women in Kerala have had a much higher standing and influence in the society. This was common among certain influential castes and is a factor in the value placed on daughters. Christian missionaries also influenced Malayali women in that they started schools for girls from poor families. Opportunities for women such as education and gainful employment often translate into a lower birth rate, which in turn, make education and employment more likely to be accessible and more beneficial for women. This creates an upward spiral for both the women and children of the community that is passed on to future generations. According to the Human Development Report of 1996, Kerala's Gender Development Index was 597; higher than any other state of India. Factors, such as high rates of female literacy, education, work participation and life expectancy, along with favourable sex ratio, contributed to it.

Kerala's sex ratio of 1.084 (females to males) is higher than that of the rest of India and is the only state where women outnumber men. While having the opportunities that education affords them, such as political participation, keeping up to date with current events, reading religious texts etc., these tools have still not translated into full, equal rights for the women of Kerala. There is a general attitude that women must be restricted for their own benefit. In the state, despite the social progress, gender still influences social mobility.

Human Development Index

As of 2015, Kerala has a Human Development Index (HDI) of 0.770, which is in the "high" category, ranking it first in the country. It was 0.790 in 2007-08 and it had a consumption-based HDI of 0.920, which is better than that of many developed countries. Comparatively higher spending by the government on primary level education, health care and the elimination of poverty from the 19th century onward has helped the state maintain an exceptionally high HDI; the report was prepared by the central government's Institute of Applied Manpower Research. However, the Human Development Report 2005, prepared by Centre for Development Studies envisages a virtuous phase of inclusive development for the state since the advancement in human development had already started aiding the economic development of the state. Kerala is also widely regarded as the cleanest and healthiest state in India.

According to the 2011 census, Kerala has the highest literacy rate (94%) among Indian states. The life expectancy in Kerala is 74 years, among the highest in India as of 2011. Kerala's rural poverty rate fell from 59% (1973–1974) to 12% (1999–2010); the overall (urban and rural) rate fell 47% between the 1970s and 2000s against the 29% fall in overall poverty rate in India. By 1999–2000, the rural and urban poverty rates dropped to 10.0% and 9.6% respectively. The 2013 Tendulkar Committee Report on poverty estimated that the percentages of the population living below the poverty line in rural and urban Kerala are 9.14% and 4.97%, respectively. These changes stem largely from efforts begun in the late 19th century by the kingdoms of Cochin and Travancore to boost social welfare. This focus was maintained by Kerala's post-independence government.

Kerala has undergone a "demographic transition" characteristic of such developed nations as Canada, Japan, and Norway;. as 11.2% of people are over the age of 60, and due to the low birthrate of 18 per 1,000. In 1991, Kerala's total fertility rate (TFR) was the lowest in India. Hindus had a TFR of 1.66, Christians; 1.78, and Muslims; 2.97. The state also is regarded as the "least corrupt Indian state" according to the surveys conducted by Transparency International (2005) and *India Today* (1997). Kerala has the lowest homicide rate among Indian states, with 1.1 per 100,000 in 2011. In respect of female empowerment, some negative factors such as higher suicide rate, lower share of earned income, child marriage, complaints of sexual harassment and limited freedom are reported.

In 2015, Kerala had the highest conviction rate of any state, over 77%. Kerala has the lowest proportion of homeless people in rural India – 0.04%, and the state is attempting to reach the goal of becoming the first "Zero Homeless State", in addition to its acclaimed "Zero landless project", with private organisations and the expatriate Malayali community funding projects for building homes for the homeless. The state was also among the lowest in the India State Hunger Index next only to Punjab. In 2015 Kerala became the first "complete digital state" by implementing e-governance initiatives.

Healthcare

Kerala, considered as being healthier than many states of the United States of America, is a pioneer in implementing the universal health care programme.

The sub-replacement fertility level and infant mortality rate are lower compared to those of other states, estimated from 12 to 14 deaths per 1,000 live births; as per the National Family Health Survey 2015-16, it has dropped to 6. However, Kerala's morbidity rate is higher than that of any other Indian state—118 (rural) and 88 (urban) per 1,000 people. The corresponding figures for all India were 55 and 54 per 1,000 respectively as of 2005.

Kerala's 13.3% prevalence of low birth weight is higher than that of many first world nations. Outbreaks of water-borne diseases such as diarrhoea, dysentery, hepatitis, and typhoid among the more than 50% of people who rely on 3 million water wells is an issue worsened by the lack of sewers. According to a study commissioned by Lien Foundation, a Singapore-based philanthropic organisation, Kerala is considered to be the best place to die in India based on the state's provision of palliative care for patients with serious illnesses.

The United Nations Children's Fund (UNICEF) and the World Health Organization designated Kerala the world's first "baby-friendly state" because of its effective promotion of breast-feeding over formulas. Over 95% of Keralite births are hospital delivered and the state also has the lowest Infant mortality rate in the country. The third National Family Health Survey ranks Kerala first in "Institutional Delivery" with 100% births in medical facilities. Ayurveda, *siddha*, and endangered and endemic modes of traditional medicine, including *kalari*, *marmachikitsa* and *vishavaidyam*, are practised. Some occupational communities such as Kaniyar were known as native medicine men in relation to the practice of such streams of medical systems, apart from their traditional vocation. These propagate via *gurukula* discipleship, and comprise a fusion of both medicinal and alternative treatments.

In 2014, Kerala became the first state in India to offer free cancer treatment to the poor, via a program called Sukrutham. People in Kerala experience elevated incidence of cancers, liver and kidney diseases. In April 2016, the *Economic Times* reported that 250,000 residents undergo treatment for cancer. It also reported that approximately 150 to 200 liver transplants are conducted in the region's hospitals annually. Approximately 42,000 cancer cases are reported in the region annually. This is believed to be an underestimate due as private hospitals may not be reporting their figures. Long waiting lists for kidney donations has stimulated illegal trade in human kidneys, and prompted the establishment of the Kidney Federation of India which aims to support financially disadvantaged patients.

RELIGION IN KERALA

Religions in Kerala are a mixture of different faiths, most significantly Hinduism, Islam and Christianity. Kerala has a reputation of being, communally, one of the most religiously diverse and cosmoplitian states in India. According to 2011 Census of India figures, 54.73% of Kerala's population are Hindus, 26.56% are Muslims, 18.38% are Christians, and the remaining 0.33% follows other religion or no religion. Various tribal people in Kerala have retained various religious beliefs of their ancestors. Hindus constitute the majority in all districts except Malappuram, where Muslims are a majority.

Religion

Religion in Kerala (2011)

Hinduism (54.73%)

Islam (26.56%)

Christianity (18.38%)

Other or none (0.32%)

In comparison with the rest of India, Kerala experiences relatively little sectarianism. According to 2011 Census of India figures, 54.73% of Kerala's residents are Hindus, 26.56% are Muslims, 18.38% are Christians, and the remaining 0.32% follow another or have no religious affiliation. Hindus constitute the majority in all districts except Malappuram, where they are outnumbered by Muslims. Kerala has the largest population of Christians in India.

The mythological legends regarding the origin of Kerala are Hindu in nature. Kerala produced several saints and movements. Adi Shankara was a religious philosopher who contributed to Hinduism and propagated the philosophy of Advaita. He was instrumental in establishing four mathasat Sringeri, Dwarka, Puri and Jyotirmath. Melpathur Narayana Bhattathiri was another religious figure who composed Narayaniyam, a collection of verses in praise of the Hindu God Krishna.

Historians do not rule out the possibility of Islam being introduced to Kerala as early as the seventh century CE. Kerala Muslims are generally referred to as the Mappilas. Mappilas are but one among the many communities that forms the Muslim population of Kerala.According to some scholars, the Mappilas are the oldest settled Muslim community in South Asia. Most of the Muslims in Kerala follow the Shâfi school of religious law while a large minority follow movements that developed within Sunni Islam. The latter section consists of majority Salafists (the Mudjahids) and the minority Islamists.

Ancient Christian tradition says that Christianity reached the shores of Kerala in AD 52 with the arrival of Thomas the Apostle, one of the Twelve Apostles of Jesus Christ. Saint Thomas Christians include Syro-Malabar Catholic, Syro-Malankara

Catholic, Jacobite Syrian, Malankara Orthodox Syrian, Marthoma Syrian, the Syrian Anglicans in the CSI and several Pentecostal and evangelical denominations. The origin of the Latin Catholic Christians in Kerala is the result of the missionary endeavours of the Portuguese Padroado in the 16th century. As a consequence of centuries of miscegenation beginning with the Portuguese, Dutch, French, British and other Europeans, there is a community of Anglo-Indians in Kerala of mixed European and Indian parentage or ancestry.

Judaism reached Kerala in the 10th century BC during the time of King Solomon. They are called Cochin Jews or Malabar Jews and are the oldest group of Jews in India.There was a significant Jewish community which existed in Kerala until the 20th century, when most of them migrated to Israel. The Paradesi Synagogue at Kochi is the oldest synagogue in the Commonwealth. Jainism has a considerable following in the Wayanad district.

Buddhism was popular in the time of Ashoka but vanished by the 12th century CE. Certain Hindu communities such as the Samantan Kshatriyas, Ambalavasis, Nairs, Thiyyas and the Muslims around North Malabar used to follow a traditional matrilineal system known as *marumakkathayam*, although this practice ended in the years after Indian independence. Other Muslims, Christians, and some Hindu castes such as the Namboothiris, most of the Ambalavasi castes and the Ezhavas followed *makkathayam*, a patrilineal system. Owing to the former matrilineal system, women in Kerala enjoy a high social status. However, gender inequality among low caste men and women is reportedly higher compared to that in other castes.

Hinduism

Several saints and movements existed. Adi Shankara was a Hindu philosopher who contributed to Hinduism and propagated philosophy of Advaita. He was instrumental in establishing four mathas at Sringeri, Dwarka, Puri and Jyotirmath. Melpathur Narayana Bhattathiri was another Brahmin religious figure who composed Narayaniyam, a collection of verses in praise of Krishna.

Vadakkunnathan Temple dedicated to Shiva at Thrissur

Various practises of Hinduism are unique to Kerala. Different cults of Shiva and Vishnu are popular in Kerala. Malayali Hindus also worship Bhagavathi as a form of Shakti. Almost every village in Kerala has its own local guardian deity, usually a goddess. Hindus in Kerala also strongly believe in power of snake gods and usually have sacred snake groves known as *Sarpa Kavu* near to their houses.

Some of the most notable temples are: Guruvayur Temple, Thrissur Vadakkunnathan Temple, Sabarimala Ayyappa Temple, Thiruvananthapuram Padmanabhaswamy Temple, Aranmula Parthasarathy Temple, Chottanikkara Temple, Chengannur Mahadeva Temple, Parassinikadavu Muthappan Temple, Chettikulangara Devi Temple, Mannarasala Temple, Chakkulathukavu Temple, Thiruvalla Sreevallabha Temple, Kaviyoor Mahadevar Temple, Parumala Panayannarkavu Temple, Sree Poornathrayesa Temple, Kodungallur Bhagavathy Temple, and Rajarajeshwara Temple. Temples in Kerala follow elaborate rituals and only priests from the Nambudiri caste can be appointed as priests in major temples. But in 2017 as per the state government's decision, the priests from backward community was appointed. These priests are assisted by a caste known as Ambalavasis.

Judaism

Judaism arrived in Kerala with spice traders, possibly as early as the 7th century BC. There is no consensus of opinion on the date of the arrival of the first Jews in India. The tradition of the Cochin Jews maintains that after 72 AD, after the destruction of the Second Temple of Jerusalem, 10,000 Jews migrated to Kerala.

The only verifiable historical evidence about the Kerala Jews goes back only to the Jewish Copper Plate Grant of Bhaskara Ravi Varman in 1000 AD. This document records the royal gift of rights and privileges to the Jewish Chief of Anjuvannam Joseph Rabban. According to some historians, St. Thomas found first converts in Kerala to his new religion amongst many of the Cochin Jews. However these Jews who accepted Christianity retained the Aramaic language once spoken by Jews in Middle East. Their descendants form the core of Syrian Christian community in Kerala. Later in the 16th century many Jews from Portugal and Spain settled in Cochin. These Jews were called *white Jews* as opposed to the native *black Jews*.

The Portuguese did not look favorably on the Jews. They destroyed the Jewish settlement in Cranganore and sacked the Jewish town in Cochin and partially destroyed the famous Cochin Synagogue in 1661. However, the Dutch were more tolerant and allowed the Jews to pursue their normal life and trade in Cochin. According to the testimony of the Dutch Jew, Mosss Pereya De Paiva, in 1686 there were 10 synagogues and nearly 500 Jewish families in Cochin.

Later Britishers too were tolerant. The Jews were protected. After the creation of the State of Israel in 1948, most Jews decided to emigrate to Israel. Most of the emigrants to Israel between 1948 and 1955 were from the community of *black Jews* and *brown Jews*; they are known as Cochini in Israel. Since the 1960s, only a few hundred Jews (mostly *white Jews*) remained in Kerala with only two synagogues open for service: the Pardesi Synagogue in Matancherry built in 1567 and the synagogue in Parur.

Jainism

Marwari Jain Temple in Kochi

Jainism arrived in Kerala around the 3rd century BC. The Jain religion was brought to the South in the third century BC by Chandragupta Maurya (321-297 BC) and the Jain saint Bhadrabahu, according to Jain traditions. They came to Sravanabelgola in Mysore. The Jains came to Kerala with the rest of the Chera immigrants starting in the sixth century.

Among the existing original Jain temples in Kerala, the most prominent is called Jainmedu, Vadakkanthara village, about 3 km from Palakkad. This temple was reportedly built by Inchanna Satur. This indicates significant population of Jains lived in Palaghat during the 15th century. Later, various members of Marwari business community built the Jain temple in Kochi.

Some historians claim many Hindu temples might have been once Jain temples. Several places in Wyanad have Jain temples: an indication that North Malabar was once a flourishing center of Jainism. Historians believe that the decline of Jainism started about the eighth century. Jainism seems to have completely disappeared from Kerala by the sixteenth century;

the foreign visitors from Europe do not mention the Jains at all.

Present day

At present, Jainism in Kerala has a small following, mainly among descendants from the original immigrating Jains, and the North Indian business community, settled in and around Kochi and Calicut.

Jains are present in significant numbers in the Wayanad district bordering the Karnataka state. Amongst the existing original Jain temples in Kerala, the most prominent is called Jainmedu, Vadakkanthara village, about 3 km from Palakkad. The remnants of the Jain temple known as *Chathurmukha Basti* is a popular destination in Manjeshwaram, Kasaragod.

Christianity

Christianity is said to have arrived in Kerala in the first century CE in AD 52 with Thomas the Apostle and is followed by 18.38% of the population. The works of scholars and Eastern Christian writings say that Thomas the Apostle visited Muziris in Kerala in the first century in 52 AD to share the gospel amongst Kerala's Jewish settlements and from this came Thomasine Christianity. The 3rd and 4th centuries saw an influx of Jewish Christians from the Middle East. However, the story of St Thomas coming to India in 52 CE has been contradicted by a recorded history. There was a Thomas who came, but he was a Syrian merchant, Thomas of Cana, and this happened around 500 or 600 CE. In-depth historical research on this topic can be found in the book by a Canadian author and a former Christian monk Ishwar Sharan and research conducted and published by Madras Courier.

Knanaya communities arrived during this time. Syriac Christians remained as an independent group, and they got their bishops from Church of the East until the advent of Portuguese and British colonialists.

The arrival of Europeans in the 15th century and discontent with Portuguese interference in religious matters fomented schism into Catholic and Orthodox communities. Further schism and rearrangements led to the formation of the other Indian Churches. Latin Rite Christians particularly on the coast of Kerala has protracted over eleven centuries and the work of evangelization was revived by the western missionaries in the 13th century. Anglo-Indian Christian communities formed around this time as Europeans and local Malayalis intermarried.

Protestantism arrived a few centuries later with missionary activity during British rule.

There are various denominations/churches exist among Christians of Kerala. In that around 61% of them are Catholics and they are Syro Malabar, Latin and Syro - Malankara catholics.

Syriac Christians in Kerala are also called Nasranis and they are Syro-Malabar Catholic Church, Malankara Orthodox Syrian Church, Malankara Jacobite Syriac Orthodox Church, Syro-Malankara Catholic Church and Marthoma Syrian Church.

Other denominations are: Church of South India, Believers Church, Pentecostal Churches, etc.

Catholic communities are Syro-Malabar Catholic Church, Latin Catholic & Syro-Malankara Catholic Church. Orthodox Communities are Malankara Orthodox Syrian Church and Malankara Jacobite Syriac Orthodox Church. All the other churches belongs to the Protestant community.

Some of the prominent churches are: St. Thomas international pilgrim church, Malayattor St. George's church, Edappally Manarcad Church, St. Mary's Church, Niranam, St. Peter and St. Paul's Church, Parumala, St. George Orthodox Church Puthuppally Pally, St. George's Church, Kadamattom, Marthoman Cathedral, Mulanthuruthy, Chengannur Pazhaya Suriyani Pally, Kozhencherry St. Thomas Marthoma Church, and Nilakkal St. Thomas Ecumenical Church

Islam

The general consensus among modern scholars is that Islam might have arrived in Kerala through Middle Eastern merchants either during the time of Prophet Mu%□ammad (c. 570 - 632 AD) itself or in the following few decades. The western coast of India was the chief centre of West Asian trading activities right from 4th century AD and by about 7th century AD, and several Middle Eastern merchants had taken permanent residence in the major port cites of Malabar Coast.

The West Asian Muslims controlled the western arm of the overseas trade to the ports of the Red Sea, and the Persian Gulf from the Malabar Coast.

The native Muslims (Mappilas and Maraikkars) dominated the trade to Myanmar and Malaysia and points east, and the Indian coastal trade (Canara, Malabar, Ceylon and Coromandel, and Bay of Bengal shores) with the Chettis from Coromandel Coast. Muslims, and Vanias from Gujarat took part in the trade with ports in Western India.

The Zamorins of Calicut (Kozhikode), the Hindu rulers of central Kerala, favoured Muslim navigators in the Arabian Sea in the late medieval period.

The arrival of the Portugueseexplorers in the late 15th century checked the then well-established and wealthy Muslim community's progress. The Portuguese Armadas attacked and looted the Muslim port towns in the Kingdom of Calicut. The Kerala Muslims - who had been depended solely on commerce - were reduced into severe economic perplexity. Some Muslim traders turned inland (South Malabar) in search of alternate occupations to commerce. The once affluent Muslim population became predominantly rural in Kerala.

By the mid-18th century the majority of the Muslims of Kerala were landless labourers, poor fishermen and petty traders, and the community was in a psychological retreat. The community tried to reverse the trend during the Mysore invasion of Malabar District of the late 18th century. The victory of the English East India Company and princely Hindu confederacy in 1792 over the Kingdom of Mysore placed the Muslims once again in economical and cultural subjection. The partisan rule of British authorities brought the land-less Mappila peasants of Malabar District into a condition of destitution, and this led to a series of uprisings (against the upper caste Hindu landlords and British administration). The series of violence eventually exploded as the infamous Mappila Uprising (1921–22). The Muslim material strength - along with modern education, theological reform, and active participation in democratic process - recovered slowly after the 1921-22 Uprising. The Muslim numbers in state and central government posts remained staggeringly low.

A large number of Muslims of Kerala found extensive employment in the Persian Gulf countries in the following years. This widespread participation in the Gulf Rush produced huge economic and social benefits for the community. Great influx funds from the earnings of Mappilas employed followed. Issues such as widespread poverty, unemployment and educational backwardness began to change. The Muslims in Kerala are now considered as section of Indian Muslims marked by recovery, change and positive involvement in the modern world.

Buddhism

Buddhism probably flourished for 200 years (650-850) in Kerala. The Paliyam Copper Plate of the Ay King, Varaguna (885-925 AD) shows that the Buddhists benefited from royal patronage in the 10th century.

Parsi (Zoroastrianism)

There were a number of Parsi families settled in Kerala, particularly around Kozhikode and Thalassery area. They practiced Zoroastrianism and even built the 160-year-old dadgah (fire temple) at Kozhikode which is still in existence. They were mostly wealthy families who immigrated during the 18th century from Gujarat and Bombay. The community included famous families such as the Hirjis or Marshalls. Some famous Malayali Parsis included the reputed Dr. Kobad Mogaseb, who was the first medical doctor from Kozhikode who graduated from London, as well as Kaikose Ruderasha who funded the Basel Evangelical Mission Parsi High School, Thalassery.

Tribal and other religious faiths

Various groups classified as tribes in Kerala still dominate various remote and hilly areas of Kerala. They have retained various rituals and practices of their ancestors despite influences of mainstream religions.

Tensions

In the 21st century various extreme religious groups have become influential in Kerala. In 2008 there was tension in streets of Kerala over introduction of a seventh standard textbook. The controversy was about a chapter in the book *Mathamillaatha Jeevan* (Life [Jeevan] without Religion). Jeevan refused to belong to any religion or caste. Various groups alleged that this book was atheistic anti-religious propaganda by ruling Left Front government.

9

Art, Architecture, Fair and Festivals

ART & CULTURE

Architecture

Kerala has made its notable contributions to the science of architecture, both secular and religious. The Tantrasamuchaya, Vastuvidya, Manushyalaya-Chandrika and Silparatna are well-known treatises on the subject. The Manushyalaya Chandrika is a work devoted to domestic architecture.

The traditional Kerala house is a quadrangular building called Nalukettu constructed strictly in accordance with the principles of Tachu Sastra (Science of Architecture). It was located in a self contained compound and was specially designed to cater to the needs of the huge tarawads of old under the Marumakkathayam (matrilineal) system. The Nalukettu was so called because it consisted of four blocks viz., the Vadakkini (northern block), Padinjattini (western block), Kizhakkini (eastern block) and Thekkini (southern block). The house was generally built of laterite plastered with Chunam and the roofs were tiled or thatched with the leaves of palmyrah or coconut trees. The wood work of the building was usually solid and beautifully carved. It may also be noted that the old palaces of Kerala represent the style of traditional domestic architecture.

The most important palaces that deserve mention are the Padmanabhapuram Palace (Kanyakumari District), the Dutch Palace at Mattancheri and the Krishnapuram Palace near Kayamkulam. In recent times domestic architecture has undergone significant changes in style and design. The houses are now built only to accommodate single households. Cement concrete houses have taken the place of the traditional houses made of brick set in either mud or lime.

The Kerala temple has a district architectural style which has been acquired as a result of a long process of evolution. The rock-cut temples are among the earliest known of the temples of Kerala and they are assigned to the period prior to 800 AD. They come mainly under two groups, the southern group and the northern group. The former includes the rock-cut temples of Vizhinjam, Madavurppara, Kottukal and Kaviyur and the latter of those of Trikkur, Irunilacode and Bhrandanpara. The Saivite cult dominated the architectural style of the temples of both these groups. Those of southern group are of Pandya origin and of the northern groups. Those of southern group are of Pandya origin and of the northern group of Pallava origin. In addition to these two groups of rock-cut temples, there is also the rock-cut temple of Kallil near Perumbavur which is at present a Bhagavathi temple, but was formerly a Jain Shrine.

The structural temple of Kerala had its origin during the 9th century A.D. The Krishna temple at Trikkulasekharapuram near Tiruvanchikulam and the Kizhthali Siva temple nearby are dated to this period on the basis of inscription and stylistic evidences. The origin of the Kandiyur Siva temple is ascribed to 823 AD on the basis of clear inscriptional evidence. In the course of centuries Kerala evolved its distinctive types of temple architecture each of which is associated with some area or other in the State. The Kerala temples have been built in square, rectangular, circular, apsidal and elliptical ground plans. The dominance of the circular shrine is a unique feature of temple architecture in Kerala. The southern half of the State has a preponderance of circular shrines. The apsidal temples lay scattered all over the west coast up to Thiruvananthapuram but there is a concentration of this type in central Kerala. The rectangular and elliptical ground plans can be seen only in a few temples in Kerala. As the rectangular plan was more suited for enshrining Vishnu as Anantasayanam, the Sri. Padmanabha Swami temple, Thiruvananthapuram, follows this type. The Siva temple at Vaikom is built on the elliptical plan. It may also be noted that majority of the Kerala temples have walls made of laterite blocks, but some made entirely of granite except the superstructure may also be in wood carvings, representing Puranic stories. The slopping roof and the lavish use of wood have also invested the Kerala temples with a distinct style of their own.

In the early period the Christians of Kerala seem to have built their churches after the model of Hindu temples, as is evidenced by the alleged action of Vasco-da-Gama in entering a Kali temple at Calicut mistaking it for a Christian church. They adopted for their churches the temple plan comprised of a four-sided sanctuary with a large pillared hall in the front. The church had also a tower which, like the Sikhara above the Garbhagriha of the temple, soared to the maximum height. The indigenous tradition which influenced church architecture continued without break till the coming of the Portuguese in 1498 AD. As part of their policy of Latinisation of the Church is Kerala, the Portuguese introduced innovations in the design of church buildings. The massive arch replaced the thick entrance door and stained glass windows were installed to allow more ventilation. The sanctum chamber (Madubaha) was attractively ornamented with statues made of wood or clay as well as with beautiful wall paintings. The first church to be built in the new style was Santo Antonio, the present St. Francis church, Cochin. The St.Francis church provided the model for the construction or more churches in India.

In modern times styles of church architecture from outside have influenced the construction of churches in Kerala. The Puthen Palli at Trichur with its arches, vaults, steeples, flying buttresses and stained glass windows has been built after Gothic style. The St.Joseph's Cathedral of the Latin Christians at Palayam, Thiruvananthapuram and the Kothamanglam church are Romanesque in their architectural style. The

St.Thomas Pontifical shrine, Kodungallur, resembles the St. Peter's Church in Rome. The new Orthodox Syrian church at Kolancherri (the church of St.Paul and St.Peter) is one of the finest specimens of modern church architecture in Kerala.

Mosque architecture which drew inspiration from Persian and Turkish tradition in north India had no influence on mosque architecture in Kerala till recently. The traditional Kerala mosque is a simple two-storied building with tiled roofs. Its outer walls are built on a basement similar to that of a Kerala temple. It has a central hall meant for prayers with corridors on all four sides. As in the case of temples and churches wood has been used profusely in the construction of the Kerala mosques. But there are a few mosques, like the Juma Masjid at Palayam, Thiruvananthapuram and Puthiya Palli at Calicut in Kerala now which are reminiscent of the Islamic style of architecture prevalent in north India.

ARCHITECTURE OF KERALA

Kerala architecture is a kind of architectural style that is mostly found in Indian state of Kerala. Kerala's style of architecture is unique in India, in its striking contrast to Dravidian architecture which is normally practiced in other parts of South India. The architecture of Kerala has been influenced by Dravidian and Indian Vedic architectural science (Vastu Shastra) over two millennia. The Tantrasamuchaya, Thachu-Shastra, Manushyalaya-Chandrika and Silparatna are important architectural sciences, which have had a strong impact in Kerala Architecture style. The Manushyalaya-Chandrika, a work devoted to domestic architecture is one such science which has its strong roots in Kerala.

The architectural style has evolved from Kerala's peculiar climate and long history of influences of its major maritime trading partners like Chinese, Arabs and Europeans.

Origins

The characteristic regional expression of Kerala architecture results from the geographical, climatic and historic factors. Geographically Kerala is a narrow strip of land lying in between western seaboard of peninsular India and confined between the towering Western Ghats on its east and the vast Arabian sea on its west. Favoured by plentiful rains due to Monsoon and bright sunshines, this land is lush green with vegetation and rich in animal life. In the uneven terrain of this region human habitation is distributed thickly in the fertile low-lands and sparsely towards the hostile highlands. Heavy rains have brought in presence of large water bodies in form of lakes, rivers, backwaters and lagoons. The climatic factors thus made its significant contributions in developing the architecture style, to counter wettest climatic conditions coupled with heavy humidity and harsh tropical summers.

History also played its own contributions to the Kerala architecture. The towering Western Ghats on its east, has successfully prevented influences of neighboring Tamil countries into present day Kerala in later times. While Western Ghats isolated Kerala to a greater extent from Indian empires, the exposure of Arabian sea on its east brought in close contacts between the ancient people of Kerala with major maritime civilizations like Chinese, Egyptians, Romans, Arabs etc. The Kerala's rich spice cultivations brought it center of global maritime trade until modern periods, helping several international powers to actively engage with Kerala as a trading partners. This helped in bring in influences of these civilisations into Kerala architecture.

History

Pre-historic era

The locational feature of Kerala has influenced the social development and indirectly the style of construction. In the ancient times the Arabian sea and the Ghats formed impenetrable barriers helping the evolution of an isolated culture of Proto-Dravidians, contemporary to the Harappan civilisation. The earliest vestiges of constructions in Kerala belong to this period dated between 3000 B.C. to 300 B.C. They can be grouped into two types – tomb cells and megaliths. The rock cut tomb cells are generally located in the laterite zones of central Kerala, for example at Porkalam, Thrissur district. The tombs are roughly oblong in plan with single or multiple bed chambers with a rectangular court in the east from where steps rise to the ground level. Another type of burial chamber is made of four slabs placed on edges and a fifth one covering them as a cap stone. One or more such dolmens are marked by a stone circle. Among the megaliths are the umbrella stones ("kudakkal"), resembling handless palm leaf umbrellas used for covering pits enclosing burial urns. Two other types of megaliths, hat stones ("thoppikkal") and menhirs ("pulachikkal") however have no burial appendages. They appear to be rather memorial stones.

The megaliths are not of much architectural significance, but they speak of the custom of the primitive tribes erecting memorials at sites of mortuary rites. These places later became the annual meeting grounds of the tribes and gave rise to occult temples of ancestral worship. While the custom of father worship can be seen in these cases, the protecting deities of the villages were always in female form, who were worshiped in open groves ("kavu"). These hypaethral temples had trees, stone symbols of Mother Goddesses or other naturalistic or animistic image as objects of worship. The continuity of this early culture is seen in the folk arts, cult rituals, worship of trees, serpents and mother images in kavus.

Influence of Buddhism and early Tamillakam architecture

The nature worship of the early inhabitants of Kerala has its parallel in serpent worship and Buddhism, in the tree worship owing to the association of Buddha's birth, revelation and preaching under a tree. This rose in parallel to the developments in the other areas of Tamilakkam during the latter stages of the Sangam period. Although sculptural relics of Buddhist images have been recovered from a few places of southern Kerala, there are, however, no extant Buddhist monuments in this region. But literary references such as the 3rd century Tamil epic Manimekhalai and Mushika vamsa, a Sanskrit epic of the eleventh century suggest the fact that Kerala had important Buddhist shrines. The most renowned of these was the

Sreemulavasa vihara with a magnificent image of Bodhisatwa Lokanatha. This shrine is believed to have been washed away by coastal erosion. In their design features some of the temples such as Siva temple at Thrissur and the Bhagavathi temple at Kodungallur are believed to be Buddhist viharas; but there is no irrefutable proof for such beliefs.

The Chuttuambalam Pavilion at Chottanikkara Temple built in classical style

The Jain monuments are more numerous in Kerala. They include rock shelters at Chitral Jain cave near Nagercoil, a rock cut temple at Kallil near Perumbavoor, and remains of structural temples at Alathoor near Palakkad and at Sultanbathery. Jainimedu Jain temple is a 15th-century Jain temple located at Jainimedu, 3 km from the centre of Palakkad.Sculptured Kerala Jaina and Dravidian figures of Mahavira, Parswanatha and other thirthankaras have been recovered from these sites. This remained a Jain temple until 1522CE before being consecrated as a Hindu temple. Sultanbathery also has the remains of a Jaina basti, known as Ganapati vattam, being an example of a cloistered temple built entirely of granite.

In spite of the absence of architectural monuments there is conclusive proof of the influence of the Buddhist school on Kerala architecture of later periods. The circular temples basically follow the shapes of the Buddhist stupas, the dome shaped mounds. The apsidal temples are modelled in the pattern of chaitya halls, the assembly halls of Buddhist monks. The chaitya window seen repeated in the decorative moulding of the thorana around the temple shrine is clearly a Buddhist motif adopted in Hindu style, according to Percy Brown. Basically thorana is a gateway provided in the palisade seen in the vertical and horizontal members of the vilakkumadam, which is a feature seen only in Kerala temples of the post-Buddhist period. In its most primitive form this construction is seen in the hypaethral temples enshrining trees and later on the outer walls of the shrines proper. With the stylistic development of the Hindu temple this form of palisade is removed from the shrine structure (srikovil) and taken as a separate edifice beyond the temple cloister (chuttambalam).

The single-storeyed temple complex at Kottarakkara in Kollam

Migrant and Dravidian influences

Buddhism was co-existent with the indigenous Dravidian cultural and social practices of Kerala. Early Tamil Sangam literature says that by the First century A.D. the Cheras all of present-day Kerala, parts of Tulunadu and Kodagu, and the

Kongu lands (present Salem and Coimbatore region). It had multiple capitals simultaneously administered by different lineages of the Family, its main capital being Vanchi, identified with the Thiruvanchikulam near Kodungallur. At this time, the two extremities of the Kerala region were administered by two Velir families. The southernmost part administered by the Ay chieftains of Thiruvananthapuram and the northernmost parts by the Nannans of Ezhilmalai. The Nannan line was a branch of the Ay originating in the Thiruvananthapuram area and both were representatives (or vassals) under the suzerainty of the Cheras (and sometimes the Pandyas or Cholas or Pallavas). Brahmanas appeared to have settled in Kerala and established their religion. The amalgamation of different cultures and religious philosophies helped to evolve the architectural styles of Kerala temples. This was highly conducive of architectural development and renovation of a large number of temples. After the decline of the Cheras several small principalities developed all over Kerala. By fifteenth century, Kerala was broadly covered by the suzerainty of four principal chieftains – Venad rulers in the south, Kochi Maharajas in the centre, Zamorins of Kozhikode in the north and Kolathiri Rajas in the extreme north. They were rulers who patronised architectural activities. It was this period, Kerala Architecture started shaping its own distinctive style. A regional character in construction incorporating the Dravidian craft skills, unique forms of Buddhist buildings, design concepts of vedic times and canonical theories of Brahmanical Agamic practices in locally available materials and suited to the climatic conditions was finally evolved in Kerala. The theory and practice of architectural construction were also compiled during this period.

Their compilations remain as classical texts of a living tradition to this day. Four important books in this area are;

- Thantrasamuchayam (Chennas Narayanan Namboodiri) and Silpiratnam (Sreekumara), covering temple architecture
- Vastuvidya (anon.) and Manushyalaya Chandrika (Thirumangalathu Sri Neelakandan), dealing with the

domestic architecture. A number of minor works in Sanskrit, Manipravalam and refined Malayalam, all based on the above texts have found popularity in Kerala with the craftsmen and professionals related with the subject.

Kerala is referred as one of the border kingdoms of the Maurya empire. It is possible that Buddhists and Jainas were the first north Indian groups to cross the borders of Kerala and establish their monasteries. These religious groups were able to practise their faith and receive patronage from the local kings to build shrines and viharas. For nearly eight centuries Buddhism and Jainism seem to have co-existed in Kerala as an important faith, contributing in its own way to the social and architectural development of the region.

Composition and structure

The circular roofs of temples are direct legacy of Buddhist influences in Ancient Kerala Architectural styles

Kerala architecture can be broadly divided into 2 distinctive areas based on their functionality, each guided by different set of principles;

- Religious Architecture, primarily patronised by temples of Kerala as well as several old churches, mosques etc.
- Domestic Architecture, primarily seen in most of the residential houses. There are distinctively styles in this area, as Palaces and large mansions of feudal lords different from houses of commoners and also marked difference exists between religious communities.

Composition

The primary elements of all structures trends to remain same. The base model is normally circular, square or rectangular plain shapes with a ribbed roof evolved from functional consideration. The most distinctive visual form of Kerala architecture is the long, steep sloping roof built to protect the house's walls and to withstand the heavy monsoon, normally laid with tiles or thatched labyrinth of palm leaves, supported on a roof frame made of hard wood and timber. Structurally the roof frame was supported on the pillars on walls erected on a plinth raised from the ground for protection against dampness and insects in the tropical climate. Often the walls were also of timbers abundantly available in Kerala. Gable windows were evolved at the two ends to provide attic ventilation when ceiling was incorporated for the room spaces.

The belief system of Vastu plays a very important role in developing architecture styles. The basic underlying belief is that, every structure built on earth has its own life, with a soul and personality which is shaped by its surroundings. The most important science which has Kerala has developed purely indigenously is Thachu-Shastra (Science of Carpentry) as the easily availability of timber and its heavy use of it. The concept of Thachu underlines that as timber is derived from a living form, the wood, when used for construction, has its own life which must be synthesised in harmony with its surroundings and people whom dwell inside it.

Materials

The natural building materials available for construction in Kerala are stones, timber, clay and palm leaves. Granite is a strong and durable building stone; however its availability is restricted mostly to the highlands and only marginally to other zones. Owing to this, the skill in quarrying, dressing and sculpturing of stone is scarce in Kerala. Laterite on the other hand is the most abundant stone found as outcrops in most zones. Soft laterite available at shallow depth can be easily cut, dressed and used as building blocks. It is a rare local stone which gets stronger and durable with exposure at atmospheric air. Laterite blocks may be bonded in mortars of shell lime, which have been the classic binding material used in traditional buildings. Lime mortar can be improved in strength and performance by admixtures of vegetable juices. Such enriched mortars were used for plastering or for serving as the base for mural painting and low relief work. Timber is the prime structural material abundantly available in many varieties in Kerala – from bamboo to teak. Perhaps the skilful choice of timber, accurate joinery, artful assembly and delicate carving of wood work for columns, walls and roofs frames are the unique characteristics of Kerala architecture. Clay was used in many forms – for walling, in filling the timber floors and making bricks and tiles after pugging and tempering with admixtures. Palm leaves were used effectively for thatching the roofs and for making partition walls.

From the limitations of the materials, a mixed mode of construction was evolved in Kerala architecture. The stone work was restricted to the plinth even in important buildings such as temples. Laterite was used for walls. The roof structure in timber was covered with palm leaf thatching for most buildings and rarely with tiles for palaces or temples. The exterior of the laterite walls were either left as such or plastered with lime mortar to serve as the base for mural painting. The sculpturing of the stone was mainly moulding in horizontal bands in the plinth portion (adhistans) whereas the carving of timber covered all elements _ pillars, beams, ceiling, rafters and the supporting brackets. The Kerala murals are paintings with vegetable dyes on wet walls in subdued shades of brown. The indigenous adoption of the available raw materials and their transformation as enduring media for architectural expression thus became the dominant feature of the Kerala style.

Structure

Structure wise, there can be two major classifications having its own specialities.

Religious architecture

Temple architecture

The variety of temples, numbering more than 2000 dotting the Kerala state has no match with any other regions of India. The temples of Kerala highly developed in strict accordance to two temple construction thesis, Thantra-Samuchayam and Sliparatnam.

While the former deals in developing structures that regulates energy flows so that positive energy flows in, while negative energy do not trend to remain retarded within the structure; whereas the latter deals in developing stone and timber architecture in such manner that each carved structure imbibe a life and personality of its own.

The standard layout of Kerala temple.

Elements and features of Kerala Temple

Sri-Kovil

The inner sanctum sanctorum where the idol of presiding deity is installed and worshiped. It shall be an independent structure, detached from other buildings with no connections and having its own roof shared with none. The Sri-kovil does not have any windows and have only one large door opening mostly towards east (sometimes it happens towards west, whereas a few temples have north facing door as its specialty, while no temples will have a south facing door).

The Srikovil may be built in different plan shapes – square, rectangular, circular or apsidal. Of these the square plan shows an even distribution throughout Kerala state. The square shape is basically the form of the vedic fire altar and strongly suggest the vedic mooring. It is categorised as the nagara style of temple in the architecutural texts. The rectangular plan is favoured for the Ananthasai Vishnu (Lord Vishnu in reclining posture) and the Sapta matrikas (Seven Mother Goddesses). The circular plan and the apsidal plan are rare in other parts of India and unknown even in the civil architecture of Kerala, but they constitute an important group of temples. The circular plan shows a greater preponderance in the southern part of Kerala, in regions once under the influence of Buddhism. The apsidal plan is a combination of the semi-circle and the square and it is seen distributed sporadically all over the coastal region. The circular temples belong to the vasara category. A variation of circle-elipse is also seen as an exception in the Siva shrine at Vaikkom. Polygonal shapes belonging to the Dravida category are also adopted rarely in temple plans but they find use as a feature of shikhara. As per the Thantrasamuchayam, every Sreekovil should be built either neutral or even sided. For the unitary temples, the overall height is taken as 13/7/ to 2 1/8 of the width of the shrine, and categorised into 5 classes as i.e.; *santhika, purshtika, yayada, achudha and savakamika* – with increasing height of the temple form. The total height is basically divided into two halves. The lower half consists of the basement, the pillar or the wall (stambha or bhithi) and the entablature (prasthara) in the ratio 1:2:1, in height. Similarly the upper half is divided into the neck (griva), the roof tower (shikhara) and the fonial (Kalasham) in the same ratio. The adisthana or foundation is generally in granite but the superstructure is built in laterite.

The roofings will be of normally taller than other temple structures.

The structural roof of the shrine is constructed as the corbelled dome of masonry; however in order to protect it from the vagaries of climate it was superposed by a functional roof, made of timber frame covered by planks and tiles. This sloping roof with its projecting caves gave the characteristic form to the Kerala temple. The fenial or Kalasham, made of copper, provided the crowning spire denoting the focus of the shrine wherein the idol was installed.

Normally the Srikovil is on a raised platform and has a flight or 3 or 5 steps to be. The steps are called Sopanapadi and on sides of the Sopanapadi, two large statues known as Dwarapalakas (Door Guards) are craved to guard the deity. As per Kerala rituals style, only main priest (Thantri) and second priest (Melshanti) only allowed to enter into Sri-kovil.

Namaskara Mandapam

The namaskara mandapa is a square shaped pavilion with a raised platform, a set of pillars and a pyramidal roof. The size of the mandapa is decided by the width of the shrine cell. The pavilion in its simplest form has four corner pillars; but larger pavilions are provided with two sets of pillars; four inside and twelve outside. Pavilions of circular, elliptical and polygonal shapes are mentioned in the texts, but they are not seen in Kerala temples. The Mandapams are used to conducting Vedic-Thantric rites.

Nalambalam

The shrine and the mandapa building are enclosed in a rectangular structure called the nalambalam. Functionally the rear and side halls of the nalambalam serves for various activities related to the ritualistic worship. The front hall is pierced with the entry, dividing it into two parts. These two halls; Agrasalas which used for feeding Brahmans, performing yagas and while Koothuambalam are used for staging temple arts such as koothu and temple murals. In few cases, Koothuambalams are separated as an individual structure outside Nalambalam.

Balithara

The Dwajasthampam or flag post of temple, in Chuttuambalam

At the entrance of Nalambalam, a square shaped raised stone altar called as Balithara can be seen. This altar is used to make ritualistic offerings to demi-gods and other spirits. Inside the Nalambalam, several small stones, called Balikallukal can be seen, meant for same purpose.

Chuttuambalam

The Goppuram or Gatehouse

The outer structure within the temple walls, is known as Chuttuambalam. Normally Chuttuambalam has main pavilion known as Mukha-Mandapam or Thala-mandapam. The Mukha-Mandapam will have the Dwajastambam (Sacred Flag-post) in center of it and has several pillars supporting mandapam. The temple is now fully enclosed in a massive wall (Kshetra-Madillukal) pierced with gate houses or gopurams. The gopuram is usually two-storeyed, which served two purposes. The ground floor was an open space generally used as a platform for temple dances such as kurathy dance or ottan thullal during festivals. The upper floor with wooden trails covering the sides functioned as a kottupura _ (a hall for drums beating). The Chuttuambalam will normally has 4 gates from outside to entrance at all sides. A stone paved walk-way will be seen around the Chuttuambalam to allow devotees circulate around the temple, which for some large temples are covered with roof supported with massive pillars on both sides. The Chuttuambalam will have Dwajavillakku or giant lamp-posts in several places, mostly in Mukha-mandapams.

Ambala-Kulam

Every temple will have a sacred temple pond or water lake located within temple complex. As per Vastu-rules, water is considered as source of positive energy and synthesis balance of all energies. Hence a temple pond or Ambala Kulam will be made available within the temple complex. The temple pond is normally used only by priests as holy bath before start of rituals as well as for various sacred rituals within the temple. In few cases, a separate pond will be constructed to allow devotees to bath before entering in temple. Today several temples have Mani-Kenar or Holy Well within the Nalambalam complex to get sacred waters for purposes of Abisekham.

Thevarapura

Normally within Nalambalam, a separate complex will be constructed for cooking foods meant to serve for the deity and distribution among devotees as holy prasadam. Such complexes are called Thevarapura, where the holy fire or Agni is invoked.

Phases of evolution

In its stylistic development, the temple architecture can be divided into three phases.

The first phase is that of rock-cut temples. This earliest form is contemporary to Buddhist cave temples. Rock-cut temples are mainly located in southern Kerala – at Vizhinjam and Ayirurpara near Tiruvananthapuram, Kottukal near Kollam and Kaviyoor near Alappuzha. Of these the one at Kaviyoor is the best example. The Kaviyoor cave temple dedicated to Siva comprises a shrine room and a spacious ardhamandapa arranged axially facing the west. On the pillared facade as well as on the walls inside the ardhamandapa are sculptured reliefs of the donor, a bearded rishi, a seated four armed Ganesh and dwarapalas. The other cave temples also have this general pattern of a shrine and an ante-room and they are associated with Siva worship. In the north similar rock-cut temples of saiva cult are seen at Trikkur and Irunilamkode in Trissoor district. Historically the cave architecture in India begins with Buddhism and the technique of rock-cut architecture in Kerala seems to be a continuation of similar works in Tamil Nadu under the Pandyas. The rock-cut temples are all dated prior to the eighth century A.D.

The structural temples appear in the second phase spanning the eighth to tenth centuries, and patronised by the Chera, Ay and Mushika chieftains. The earliest temples had a unitary shrine or a srikovil. In rare cases a porch or ardhamandapa is seen attached to the shrine. A detached namaskara mandapa is generally built in front of the srikovil. A quadrangular building, nalambalam that encloses the srikovil, the namaskara mandapa, balikkal (altar stones) etc. became part of this basic plan composition of the Kerala temple started emerging in this phase.

The middle phase of the evolution of the temples is characterised by the emergence of the sandhara shrine. In the unitary shrine of the earlier type, Nirendhara (single level of srikovil), there is a cell with a single doorway to the cell. But in the sandhara shrine the cell has twin wells leaving a passage in between them. Also there are often four functional doors on all the four cardinal directions and pierced windows to provide subdued light in the passage. Sometimes the functional door on the sides and the rear are replaced by pseudo doors.

The concept of the storeyed temple is also seen in this phase. The tower of the shrine rises to the second storey with a separate upper roof forming a dwitala (two-storeyed) temple. There is a unique example of thrithala (three-storeyed temple) is at Shiva shrine at Peruvanam with lower two storeys of square plan and the third storey of octagonal form.

In the last phase, (1300–1800 A.D.) the stylistic development reached its apogee with greater complexity in the temple layout and elaboration of detail. The vilakkumadam, the palisade structure fixed with rows of oil lamps is added beyond the nalambalam as an outer ring. The Altar stone is also housed in a pillared structure, the Balikkal mandapam in front of the agrasala (valiyambalam). A deepastambham and dwajasthambham (the lamp post and flag mast) are added in front of the balikkal mandapam.

Within the prakara but beyond the vilakkumadam, stood the secondary shrines of parivara devathas (sub-gods) in their assigned positions. These were unitary cells, in general, though in a few cases each became a full-fledged shrine as in the case of Krishna shrine in the Siva temple at Tali, Kozhikode. The last phase culminated in the concept of the composite shrines. Herein two or three shrines of equal importance are seen cloistered inside a common nalambalam. The typical example of this is the Vadakkumnatha temple at Trissoor, where in three shrines dedicated to Siva, Rama and Sankaranarayana are located inside the nalambalam. The prakara may also contain temple tanks, vedapadhasalas and dining halls. Paradoxically some shrines have not a single secondary shrine, the unique example being the Bharatha shrine at Irinjalakuda.

A significant feature of big temple complexes is the presence of a theatre hall known as Koothambalam, meant for dance, musical performance and religious recitals. This is a unique edifice of Kerala architecture, distinct from the natyasabha or natyamandir seen in north Indian temples of this period. Koothambalam is a large pillared hall with a high roof. Inside the hall is a stage structure called as Rangamandapam for the performances. The stage as well as the pillars are ornately decorated. Visual and acoustic considerations are incorporated in the layout of the pillars and construction details so that the performances can be enjoyed by the spectators without discomfort and distortion. The Koothambalam design seems to have been based on the canons given in the Natyasastra of Bharata Muni.

In the southernmost Kerala, the temple architecture was also influenced by the developments in Tamil Nadu. At Sucheendram and Tiruvananthapuram this influence is clearly seen. Herein lofty enclosures, sculptured corridors and ornate mandapas all in granite stone practically conceal the view of the original main shrine in typical Kerala style. The entrance tower, Gopuram also rises to lofty heights in a style distinct from that of the humble two-storeyed structure seen elsewhere.

Technically the most important feature of the temple architecture of Kerala is the construction technique using a dimensional standardisation. The nucleus of the temple plan is the shrine containing the garbhagrhiha cell. The width of this cell is the basic module of the dimensional system. In plan composition, the width of the shrine, the open space around it, the position and sizes of the surrounding structures, are all related to the standard module. In vertical composition, this dimensional co-ordination is carried right up to the minute construction details such as the size of the pillars, wall plates, rafters etc. The canonical rules of the proportionate system are given in the treatises and preserved by the skilled craftsmen. This proportionate system has ensured uniformity in architectural style irrespective of the geographical distribution and scale of construction.

Temple architecture is a synthesis of engineering and decorative arts. The decorative elements of the Kerala temples are of three types – mouldings, sculptures and painting. The moulding is typically seen in the plinth where in horizontal hands of circular and rectangular projections and recesses in varying proportions help to emphasize the form of the adisthana. Occasionally this plinth is raised over a secondary platform – upapeedam – with similar treatment. Mouldings are also seen in the mandapam, the hand rails of the steps (sopanam) and even in the drain channel (pranala) or the shrine cell.

The sculptural work is of two types. One category is the low relief done on the outer walls of the shrine with masonry set in lime mortar and finished with plaster and painting. The second is the sculpturing of the timber elements – the rafter ends, the brackets, the timber columns and their capitals, door frames, wall plates and beams. Decorative sculptural work is seen best in the ceiling panels of the mandapas. Exquisite lacquer work in brick red and black colour was adopted for turned columns of timber. Metal craft was also used in sculpturing idols, motifs, cladding and fenials. All sculptural works were done strictly according to the canons of proportions (ashtathala, navathala and dasathala system) applicable to different figures of men, gods and goddesses, prescribed in texts.

The painting was executed in organic pigments on walls when the plaster was still wet – in soft subdued colours, making them into a class designated as Kerala murals. The theme of these paintings is invariably mythological and the epic stories unfold as one circumambulates around the temple. The moulding, sculpture and painting are also taken in vertical compositions to emphasise the different storey heights, projecting dormer windows which break the sloping roof and the crowning finial. But in all cases the decoration is secondary to the structural form. The sculptured walls are protected by the projecting caves which keep them in shade in sharp contrast with the bright sunlit exterior. This helps to impart the overall perceptual experience of light and shade revealing details only gradually to a keen observer.

Islamic architecture

The Mithqalpalli in Kozhikode is a classic example of Kerala's native Mosque style with gabled roofs, sloped wooden window panels and without minarets

The Arabian Peninsula, the cradle of Islam also had direct trade contact with Kerala coast from very early times, as far as the time of Muhammad or even before. As local Muslim legends and tradition goes, a Chera King embraced Islam and made a voyage to Mecca. In his return trip accompanied by many Islamic religious leaders including Malik ibn Dinar, he fell sick and died. But he had given introductory letters for the party to proceed to Kodungallur. The visitors came to the port and handed over the letter to the reigning King who treated the guests with all respect and extended facilities to establish their faith in the land. The king arranged for the artisans to build the first mosque at Kodungallur near the port and ear-marked the area around it for their settlement. The original mosque has undergone extensive repairs, but the traces of the original construction are seen in the plinth, the columns and the roof which are in the old traditional styles of Hindu temples.

An example of traditional Kerala style of Mosque at Thazhathangady in Kottayam

Undoubtedly Islam spread in Kerala through the migration of new groups from Arabian Peninsula and the gradual conversion of native population in the permissive and all accommodating Indian cultural ethos and social set up of Kerala. By twelfth century AD there were at least ten major settlements of Muslims distributed from Kollam in the south to Mangalore in the north each centered on the mosque. Also a branch of the ruling kingdom at Arakkal, Kannur was converted to Islam. The primacy in trade, the spread of the faith and the experience of the sea made Muslims a prominent class and dear to the rulers, especially of the Kozhikode Zamorins. Consequently, by fifteenth century Islamic constructions reached considerable heights.

The mosque architecture of Kerala exhibits none of the features of the Arabic style nor those of the Indo-Islamic architectures of the imperial or provincial school in north India. The reason for this is not far to seek. The work of mosque construction was done by the local Hindu artisans under instructions of the Muslim religious heads who wanted to erect the places of worship. The models for places of worship were only Hindu temples or the theatre halls ("koothambalam") and these models are to be adapted for the new situations. The early mosques in Kerala consequently resemble the traditional building of the region. Arabic style of architecture was introduced to the Malabar area of present-day Kerala, during the period of occupation by Hyder Ali and later by Tipu Sultan during the eighteenth century. A large number of temples were converted to mosques during this period as evidenced by the traditional Kerala style of these structures.

In plan the mosque comprises a large prayer hall with a mihrab on the western wall (since Mecca is west to Kerala) and covered verandah all around. Generally it has a tall basement similar to the adhistana of the Brahmanical temple and often the columns are treated with square and octagonal section as in mandapa pillars. The walls are made of laterite blocks. The arch form is seen only in one exceptional case for the mosque at Ponnani and nowhere else in the early ten mosques of the land. Wood was used extensively in superstructure for the construction of ceiling and roof. The roof in many cases is covered with sheets of copper incorporating fenials in the ridge, completing the form of temple shikhara with the stupi. At Tanur the Jama Masjid even has a gate built in the manner of temple gopuram, covered with copper sheeting. This mosque itself is a three-storeyed building with tiled roof crowned by five fenials.

The pulpit in the mosque present the best example of wood carvings associated with Islamic architecture of Kerala. The Jama Masjid at Beypore and Mithqal Mosque at Kozhikode have the pulpit (mimbar) built by the ship masters of the Arab vessels.

All other construction work was done by the same local craftsmen who were building the Hindu temples and residences. The Arabic tradition of simplicity of plan had perhaps combined itself with the indigenous construction techniques giving rise to the unique style of mosque architecture, not found anywhere else in the world. In contrast the Indo-Islamic architecture drew its inspiration from the Turkish and Persian traditions and created highly ornamental style in the north India. The typical Kerala mosques are seen at Kollampalli, near Kollam, Panthalayani near Koyilandy, Kozhikode, Tanur, Ponnani and Kasargode as well as in most old Muslim settlements. The austere architectural features of the old mosques are however in the process of being replaced in recent times by Islamic architecture. The use of arcuated forms, domes and minar-minarets of the imperial school of Indo-Islamic architecture are being projected as the visible symbols of Islamic culture. The Jama Masjid at Palayam, Thiruvananthapuram is the classic example of this new trend. Similar structures are coming up all over Kerala in the modification of old mosques during the last decades.

Perhaps the influence of Arabic style of Kerala construction is seen in a subtle manner in the secular architecture of Muslims. The bazar streets lined by buildings on both sides, the upper floor living rooms with view windows to the streets, the wooden screens used to provide privacy and shade in the verandahs (specially of upper floors) etc., are a few features superposed on the traditional construction. These built forms would have been modelled in the pattern of the houses in Arab countries (such as Egypt, Basra (present day Iraq) and Iran) having contact with this region. This trend is most conspicuous in market towns such as Kozhikode,

Thalassery, Kasaragode etc. But basically the Muslim domestic architectures at large follow the traditional Hindu styles. Both "ekasalas" and "nâlukettus" are seen adopted for this. These buildings with extensive alindams and verandahs are also seen generally surrounding the mosques in Muslim settlements.

Church architecture

The Kadamattom Church near Muvattupuzha, is one of the oldest churches in Kerala, built in pure Kerala style.

The evolution of the church architecture of Kerala springs from two sources – the first from the work of Apostle St. Thomas and the Syrian Christians and second from the missionary work of European settlers.

The tradition has it that St. Thomas who landed in Muziris in 52 AD had seven churches built in Kerala at Kodungallur, Chayil, Palur, Paravur-Kottakkavu, Kollam, Niranom and Kothamangalam, but none of these Syrian churches are now extant.

It is possible that some of the temples were adapted as Syrian churches for services by the population who got converted into Syriac Christianity by St. Thomas. For example, the present Palur Syrian church has preserved the abhisheka patra (the letter of intonation) and certain shaiva symbols as the relics of the old church which is said to have been a Hindu shrine adapted for Christian worship.

Historical evidences suggest that the first wave of Christianity came from Edessa, Persia in the fourth century A.D. owing to the persecution of Syrian Christians in the Persian empire. According to the narration of Byzantine monk Cosmas, Kerala had many churches by sixth century A.D. According to the inscription of the times of Stanu Ravi by ninth century, Syrian Christian communities enjoyed many rights and privileges. They also played a vital role in trade and commerce. The domestic buildings of the Syrian Christians were akin to the native architecture.

But original Syrians who had migrated to Kerala had brought with them some of the West Asian conventions in church architecture. Consequently, churches with regular chancel and nave began to be built and there evolved a distinctive style of church architecture. The peculiar feature of this style was the ornamental gable facade at the nave end, surmounted by a cross. An entry porch (shala) in front of the nave was another feature of these early shrines. The baptistry was a small chamber inside the nave near the entrance. Belfries were built on one side of the nave, but in smaller churches the bell was hung in an opening in the nave gable.

Kottakkavu Mar Thoma Syro-Malabar Pilgrim Church, North Paravur is a mixture of Syrian, Kerala and European architecture

Elements of Kerala church architecture

Unlike Kerala temples, there is no uniform or standard layout for all churches of Kerala. Rather most of churches have different set to architecture according to various sects and their traditions apart from experimentation of new designs. Still most of churches, particularly Saint Thomas Christian churches of Kerala, do share several common features.

The church had a gable roof extending to the chancel, the most sacred part of the church and the sacristy by its side. The tower over the chancel soared higher than the roof of the nave similar to the shikhara over the garbhagriha in a Hindu temple. The residence of the priest and the parish hall were located on one side of the church and the cemetery was on the other side.

In their external feature Syrian churches retained some of the indigenous features of the Hindu style. The church and the ancillary buildings were enclosed in a massive laterite wall.

There was an open cross in front of the main entrance on a granite basement in the model of balikkal, the altar stone. A church also had the flag mast, (the dwajastambha) in front. In the Orthodox Syrian church at Chengannur, Peter and Paul occupy the place of dwarapalas, the guarding deities of a Hindu shrine. Sometimes a gateway like the temple gopuram with a kottupura or music room on the upper storey was also provided. The Marth Mariam church at Kuravilangad, originally built in

345 A.D had undergone renovations several times. The church has a rich collection of old relics including an idol of Virgin Mary and a cross carved in granite. The Knanaya Valiapally of Kaduthuruthy is another old church with the biggest cross formed in a single granite piece. The Valiapally of Piravom is also another old church with old Persian writings.

Wood carving and mural paintings, the two decorative media of temples are seen to be adopted in ancient churches also. A famous piece of wooden carving is a large panel depicting the last supper in St. Thomas church, Mulanthuruthy.

The All Saints church at Udayamperur has a beam resting on wooden mouldings of heads of elephants and rhinoceros. Floral figures, angels and apostles are the usual motifs of mural paintings. This form of decoration had continued in later churches as well. In St. Sebastian's church at Kanjoor a mural even depicts the fight between British and Tippu Sultan.

Colonial influences in church architecture

The Portuguese were the first to introduce European styles in the church architecture of Kerala, followed by Dutch and British.

The first church of this type in India was built by the Franciscan missionaries in 1510 A.D. at Fort Kochi. It is a small unpretentious building of the medieval Spanish type. When Vasco De Gama died in Kochi in 1524 his body was interned in this church and later removed to Lisbon in 1538.

The church thus came to be known as Vasco De Gama's church. It was later seized by the Dutch and was used for reformed services. Later with British occupation of Kochi it became an Anglican church and presently it belongs to church of south India.

The Portuguese had introduced many innovations in the Kerala churches. For the first time, the dominating tower above the altar, which was the adaptation from temple architecture, was discarded. Inside the church, the granite images were not favoured owing to their association with the Hindu art; instead images of Saints made of wood were used to adorn the riches.

Generally pulpits were erected and altar pieces were ornamented in an impressive manner. Ceilings and walls were painted with religious themes in the style of European masters. Pointed and rounded arches were introduced and stained glass windows were installed.

The subsequent development in church architecture in the British period also saw the introduction of a new church design. In place of the rectangular Basilican plan the cross shaped plan became increasingly popular especially in places where large congregation had to be accommodated.

Apart from the obvious symbolism of the cross, this plan is more suited for better visibility of the altar from all points in the church. Further, sufficient space was now available at the transepts for additional altars for services by several priests on important occasions like Christmas.

In the external features the central tower or rather the Roman dome now comes at the centre of the transept imparting a classic form of European architecture.

Also on either side of the main entrance in the front, rose towers to serve as belfries. In the treatment of the exterior, typical features of European church architecture were introduced – the Gothic arches, the pilasters and buttresses, the rounded openings, the classic mouldings and stained glass windows making the whole composition completely different from the native architecture.

Depending on the period of construction, one can also distinguish between the churches done in the simplicity of Gothic style as in the Palayam church, Tiruvananthapuram, and the luxury of renaissance style as in the church of Our Lady of Dolorous at Trissoor.

Modern trends in church architecture

While the character of church architecture is generally identified with the form evolved in the medieval times, the modernistic trends in adapting new plan shapes and structural forms are visible in the Kerala scene as well. This circular plan shape with domical shell roof has been adopted in the Christ

College church at Irinjalakkuda. The Cathedral church of Archbishop of Varapuzha at Ernakulam is a soaring hyperbolic paraboloid in reinforced concrete with a bold expression in sharp contrast with all traditional forms. Perhaps experimentation in religious architecture is mostly manifested in church architecture as compared to that in temples or mosques which more or less adhere to old evolved forms.

Jewish architecture

The architectural scene of Kerala was influenced by many socio-cultural groups and religious thoughts from foreign lands. The sea board had promoted trade contacts with maritime nations such as Israel, Rome, Arabia and China even prior to the dawn of the Christian era.

The trade contact would have paved the way of establishing settlements near the old port towns and gradually spreading in the interior. During the time of the second Chera Kingdom, the old port city of Makotai (Kodungallur) had different parts occupied by these groups.

For example, the cultural contact of Jews with Kerala predates the time of Solomen and by fifteenth century there were Jewish settlements in Kodungallur, Kochi and other coastal towns.

The most important Jewish settlement is seen at Kochi near the Mattancherry palace. Their residential buildings resemble the Kerala type in their external appearance; nevertheless they are of a different plan concept. The ground floor rooms are used as shops or warehouses and the living rooms are planned on the first floor. The frontage of the building about the streets and the sides are continuous with adjoining buildings in the pattern of the row houses. An important historic monument of the Jew town is the Synagogue. It is a simple tall structure with a sloping tile roof but it has a rich interior with hand painted tiles from Canton, China and ancient chandeliers from Europe. This religious structure built for worship according to Judaism stands in contrast with the temples of Hindus. Jewish community however did not influence the architecture of Kerala.

Domestic architecture

Intricate wood carvings & chuttu verandah in Kerala architecture

The Sree Padmanabhapuram Palace represents the most classic Kerala domestic architecture. It is also the world's largest wooden palace made on sloping roofs, granite and rosewood-teak wood work combinations

The evolution of domestic architecture of Kerala followed closely the trend of development in temple architecture. The primitive models were huts made of bamboo frame thatched with leaves in circular, square or rectangular plain shapes. The rectangular shape with a hipped roof appears to have been finally evolved from functional consideration.

Structurally the roof frame was supported on the pillars on walls erected on a plinth raised from the ground for protection against dampness and insects in the tropical climate. Often the walls were also of timbers abundantly available in the land. The roof frame consisted of the bressumer or wall plate which supported lower ends of the rafters, the upper ends being connected to the ridge. The weight of the rafters and the roof covering created a sage in the ridge when the ridge piece was made of flexible materials like bamboo.

This sage however remained as the hall-mark of roof construction even when strong timber was used for the roof frame. Further gable windows were evolved at the two ends to provide attic ventilation when ceiling was incorporated for the room spaces. This ensured air circulation and thermal control for the roof. The lower ends of the rafters projected much beyond the walls to shade the walls from the sun and driving rain. The closed form of the Kerala houses was thus gradually evolved from technical considerations. One can see the striking similarity of this form with the temple structure. The plinth, the lower most part is still called adisthana, though it is plain or less ornate. The sthambas or pillars and bhithis or walls are again of simple shape with no projection or recesses. The main door faces only in one cardinal direction and the windows are small and are made like pierced screens of wood. The rectangular plan is usually divided into two or three activity rooms with access from a front passage. The projecting caves cover a verandah all round. By tenth century, the theory and practice of domestic architecture were codified in books such as Manushyalaya Chandrika and Vastu vidya. This attempt standardised the house construction suited to different socio-economic groups and strengthens the construction tradition among the craftsmen. The traditional craftsman, specially carpenters, preserved the knowledge by rigidly following the canonical rules of proportions of different elements as well as the construction details to this day.

Basically the domestic architecture of Kerala follows the style of detached building; row houses seen in other parts of India are neither mentioned in Kerala texts nor put up in practice except in settlements (sanketam) occupied by Tamil or Konkini Brahmans. In its most developed form the typical Kerala house is a courtyard type – nalukettu. The central courtyard is an outdoor living space which may house some object of cult worship such as a raised bed for tulssi or jasmine (mullathara). The four halls enclosing the courtyard, identical to the nalambalam of the temple, may be divided into several rooms for different activities such as cooking, dining, sleeping, studying, storage of grains etc. Depending on the size and importance of the household the building may have one or two upper storeys (malika) or further enclosed courtyard by repetition of the nalukettu to form ettukettu (eight halled building) or a cluster of such courtyards.

Nalukettu

Nâlukettu is the traditional homestead of Tharavadu where many generations of a matrilineal family lived. These types of buildings are typically found in the Indian state of Kerala. The traditional architecture is typically a rectangular structure where four blocks are joined together with a central courtyard open to the sky. The four halls on the sides are named Vadakkini (northern block), Padinjattini (western block), Kizhakkini (eastern block) and Thekkini (southern block). The architecture was especially catered to large families of the traditional tharavadu, to live under one roof and enjoy the commonly owned facilities of the marumakkathayam homestead.

Elements of Nalukettu

Padippura

It is a structure containing a door forming part of Compound wall for the house with a tiled roof on top. It is the formal entry to the compound with the house. At present the door is not there as car will have to enter the house through the entry. Still tiled roof is provided preferably with a traditional type lamp below the roof. Instead of door of entry, we now have the Gate

Poomukham

It is the prime portico soon after steps to the house. Traditionally it has a slope tiled roof with pillars supporting roof. Sides are open. In the earlier days, the head of the family called *Karanavar* used to sit here in a reclining chair with thuppal kolambi (Spittoon) by the side of chair. This chair will have long rails on either side where the Karanavar will keep his legs raised for comfortable rest

Chuttu verandah

From the Poomukham, a verandah to either side in front of the house through open passage called Chuttu Verandah. Chuttu verandah will have hanging lights in equal distance hanging from its slope roof.

Charupady

By the side of Chuttu verandah and Poomukham, wooden benches with carved decorative resting wooden pieces for resting the back are provided. This is called Charupady. Traditionally the family members or visitors used to sit on these charupady to talk

Ambal Kulam (Pond)

At the end of Chuttu verandah there used to be a small pond built with rubble on sides where lotus or Ambal used to be planted. The water bodies are maintained to synthesised energy flow inside.

Nadumuttom

Traditionally Nadumuttom or central open courtyard is the prime center the Nalukettu. There is an open area usually square shaped in the exact middle of the house dividing the house in its four sides. Due to this four side division of the house by having a Nadumuttom. Similarly there was Ettu kettu and Pathinaru kettu which are quite rare with two and four Nadumuttom respectively.

Nadumuttom will be normally open to sky, allowing sunshine and rains to pour in. This is to allow natural energies to circulate within the house and allow positive vibrance within. A thulsi or tree will be normally planted in center of Nadumuttom, which is used to worship. Architecturally the logic is allow tree to act as a natural air purifier.

Pooja Room

Pooja room should preferably be in the North East corner of the house. Idols can be placed facing east or west and the person praying can face west or east respectively. At present, wooden panelling is done on Pooja room walls and there is a standard design for Pooja room which can be given to clients interested in having traditional Pooja room

Key features

The whole being protected with a compound wall or fence. An entrance structure (padippura) may also be constructed like the gopuram of a temple. This may contain one or two rooms for guests or occasional visitors who are not entertained in the main house. The position and sizes of various buildings, including the location of trees and paths within the compound wall were to be decided from the analysis of the site according to the prescriptions in the classic texts. This analysis involved the concept of vastupurusha mandala wherein the site (vastu) was divided into a number of grids (padam) occupied by different deities (devatha) and appropriate grids were chosen to house the suspicious structures. The site planning and building design was done by learned vishwakarma sthapathis (master builders) who synthesised the technical matters with astrological and mystical sciences.

There are numerous buildings of the nalukettu type in different parts of Kerala, though many of them are in a poor state of maintenance. Changing socio-economic conditions have split up the joint-family system centered on the large nalukettu. The Kailasa mandiram at Kottakkal belonging to the Arya

Vaidyasala is a standing example of a three-storeyed nalukettu complex. Of the best preserved examples of this type are Mattancherry palace at Kochi and the taikottaram of the Padmanabhapuram palace near Kanyakumari.

Nalukettu type buildings are also seen in many villages and towns, occupied by prominent people. The humbler buildings of the population are however smaller and simpler in form but basically derived from the nalukettu. Nalukettu is a combination of four halls along four cardinal directions, centered on the courtyard or anganam one may build any one of the four halls (Ekasala), a combination of two (Dwisala) or a complex of three (Thrisala) depending on the needs. The most commonly found type in Kerala is the Ekasala facing east or north. Being located on the western and southern sides of the anganam they are referred as western hall (padinjattini) and southern hall (thekkini) respectively.

The core unit of Ekasala consists of generally three rooms connected to a front passage. The central room is used as prayer room and grain store and the two side rooms are used as living rooms. The core unit may be raised to an upper storey with a steep stair located in the front passage. The building may also be extended horizontally on all the four sides adding alindams or side rooms for activities such as cooking, dining, additional sleeping rooms, front hall for receiving guests etc.The Chappamattam Tharavadu at Chirakkadavu is a classical example of extended Ekasala. If needed Ekasala may also be provided with ancillary buildings for cattle keeping, barn, bathing rooms near tanks, outhouse for guests, gate house etc. By such extension the building may become much larger than a Nalukettu in space, but it is still categorised as Ekasala with reference to its core unit.

Vastuvidya texts prescribe the dimensions of different house types suitable for different classes. They also give the proportional system of measurements for different parts of the building all based on the perimeter (chuttu) of the core unit. The scientific basis of this dimensional system is yet to be enquired by modern studies; however the system appears to be well founded on traditional computational methods and rigidily adhered to all sizes of buildings. All over Kerala and specially in villages where the building activity is still carried out under the control of traditional stapathis, the system is still a living practice, though it has started disappearing under the impact of 'modern architecture'.

Types of Nalukettu

Nalukettus can be differentiated based on structure kind as well as based on caste of its occupants.

Based on structure

Nalukettus are primarily differentiated based on their structure. Traditionally Nalukettu has one courtyard with 4 blocks/halls constructed around it in cardinal directions. However some Nalukettus have 2 courtyards, which are known as Ettukettu (8 Blocked structure) as they have altogether 8 blocks in cardinal directions. Some super structures have 4 courtyards, which then are known as Patinarukettu (16 blocked structure).

While Nalukettus and Ettukettus are more common, Pathinarukettu are extremely rare, due to its enormous size.

Likewise Nalukettus can be differentiated based on their height and number of floors. Some Nalukettus are single-storeyed and made with wood completely. Other Nalukettus are two-storeyed or sometimes even three-storeyed and have laterite-and-clay mixture as walls.

Based on caste

The actual term used for Nalukettus differ based on caste and social status of its occupants.

- For Nairs and other Feudal lords, most of the Nalukettus are referred as Tharavadu
- For Upper Ezhava and Thiyya classes, their Nalukettus are referred as Madom, Meda and Tharavadu
- For Kshatriya, their residences are referred as Kovilakoms and Kottarams

- For Syrian Christians, their residences are referred as Medas and Veedus
- For Nambudiri communities, their residences are referred as Illams

Public structures architecture

Unlike other parts of India as well as outside, most of the administrative functions under monarchical days were conducted within premises of palace complexes. Hence the concept of independent secular public structures and its architecture evolved towards later part of the 17th century, particularly due to the contributions made by colonial powers in Kerala.

Portuguese were the first, to introduce independent office complexes which stand away from residential quarters. This was out of necessity to make warehouses and its related offices away from residential apart as safety precautions.The public architectural development in Kerala was highly influenced by the European style during seventeenth to nineteenth century. The influence of the Portuguese and Dutch was most predominant in the initial stages. A Portuguese architect Thomas Fernandez is credited with the construction of forts, warehouses and bungalows at Kochi, Kozhikode and Kannur. The projecting balconies, Gothic arches and cast-iron window grill work are a few of the features passed on to Kerala architecture by the Portuguese construction. Portuguese have commissioned more than 2000 office and warehouse complexes in Fort Cochin area, apart from several European styled castles and private residential villas.

By eighteenth century British style was being popularised in the land as a result of a large number of modern constructions directly carried out by the British rulers on the one hand and the fashion for things Western by the princely class and the rich on the other. The architectural work was guided by the officers and engineers whose knowledge of the architectural style was essentially restricted to the classic books on renaissance architects – Vitruvious, Alberti & Palladio and executed by indigenous knowledge of traditional masons and carpenters recruited for the work. In a sense it was a compromise of antique craft and neo-classical construction needs.

A notable feature of the early European work in India was a tendency to demonstrate military, political and cultural superiority of the west. The Greek and Roman antiquity was considered as the richest heritage of the west and the same was emphasised in the classic orders of pillars with triangular pediments, arches and domes for public buildings, town halls, hospitals, railway stations, colleges etc. Expression of dominance was inbuilt in Doric and Ionian columns of large dimension. At the same time the purity of classic Western style gave way to the effect of style by mixing different types of columns in all sorts of buildings. For example, Corinthian columns were used mixed with Doric order in public buildings as well as residences.

This trend was however moderated very much in Kerala owing to the limitations of materials and climate.

For the masonry work the media of Indo-European work remained the laterite and lime plastering. The potentiality of exposed laterite was explored in many cases from railway quarters to government offices (e.g. old Huzur office – Collectorate, Kozhikode). Lime plastering and finishing was transferred from the interior walls of places to the exterior of buildings also to create the superwhite buildings of marble cult. The old pan tiles were replaced by Mangalore pattern tiles and flat tiles. The roof frame of traditional type was changed to trussed roof-using King post and Queen post trusses, making it possible to span large areas.

Perhaps the adaptations of European style to the climatic needs and the synthesis with traditional style are best seen in the bungalow architecture. The comfort requirement in the hot humid climate prompted the European settlers to go in for buildings with large rooms with high ceiling with verandah all around. For upper floor rooms balconies were adopted as a necessary feature, originating from the Portuguese construction. The portico, the shaded spot for passage from one building to another was added. The solid wooden shutter of doors and windows underwent change to ribbed elements – Venetian blades – permitting air circulation and providing privacy simultaneously. By 1800 glazed panels came into vogue and semicircular fan light over doors and windows became fashionable features of domestic buildings. Brick arches, terracota pieces and exposed brick work in various bonding patterns became popular. With larger number and bigger size of windows, pediments or projections supported by ornamental brackets and column decoration for protecting the window opening from rain and sun also were introduced. Cast iron fences, stair balustrades and iron grills, made in England, were used to complete the bungalow architecture.

Excellent examples of this synthesis are seen in the Napier museum at Tiruvananthapuram, and many government bungalows. In fact many of these features were smoothly adopted by the native builders to the extent that they are considered by most as traditional elements. The works of Public Works Departments have helped to spread this type of construction all over Kerala. Further the introduction of engineering education with emphasis to the western practice of construction have promoted this trend practically displacing traditional design methods.

Environmentally friendly architecture

British Architect Laurie Baker has contributed to the Modern Architecture era in Kerala by introducing a blend of British Brick-based and Vernacular Architecture style to influence the contemporary Architects. Kerala boasts of many beautiful buildings created by Architects like Laurie baker, and Architects, who were influenced by him. Banasura Hill Resort is an other innovative Architectural design where the traditional cost effective principles of Indian Architecture were used in an exemplary way.

FAIRS AND FESTIVALS IN KERALA

The God's Own Country, Kerala is the ultimate land of fairs and festivals. Although the land draws more fame from the emerald backwaters and Ayurveda, fairs and festival in Kerala are also alluring tourist attractions. A tour during the time of fairs and festivals is the best way to experience a destination with rich cultural heritage. The same holds true for Kerala too.

One of the most popular festivals in Kerala is of course the snake boat race. Apart from that there are several temple festivals that are held in different parts of Kerala. Like anywhere else in India, myths and legends have a lot to do in the origin and development of the fairs and festivals in Kerala.

Traditionally, the elephants play an important role in the life and culture of Kerala. The same is best manifested during the fairs and festivals in Kerala. Ornately decorated elephants in front of the temples offer a spectacle to behold.

Fairs and festivals in Kerala also give the best opportunity to display the traditional performing arts and delicious cuisine of the land.

Onam

Onam is the largest or the traditional ten day harvest festival of Kerala celebrated in the month of August - September (starting of the Chingam month of Malayalam Calendar) with much grandeur and fanfare. No wonder the king of festivals in Kerala "Onam" continue its charm and rituals from first to ten days, but first day, "Atham" and tenth day, "Thiruonam" are most significant of all.

The celebration of Onam is commonly noted with flower decorations or fine designs of carpets of flowers in front of the houses, elephant processions, classical and folk music concerts, classical and folk dance performances or Kathakali dances, cultural spectacle or contests, water carnivals, fireworks, sports, games, Vallamkali - the famous snake boat race, superb feast called Ona Sadya and much more which enthrall not only Keralites or Indian tourists as well as foreign tourists to visit Kerala and be a part of Onam. Because of its grandeur or fame, rich culture and heritage and colourfulness the state government promotes Onam festival internationally in a huge way and celebrates "Tourist Week" for Kerala at the time of Onam celebration.

Would you like to find out when Onam is in coming years and where to best visit them? Browse this Onam Celebration in Coming Years/Spectacular Destinations for Onam Celebration.

Vishu

Vishu festival is the astrological New Year of Kerala celebrated in the month of April (first day of Malayalam month - Medam) is treated as good, lucky or fortunate day. There are many traditional vibrant rituals and customs performed by Keralites on Vishu day with fun, pleasure and happinessbut some of the major glimpse of Vishu festival are:Vishukani, Vishukaineetam and Vishu pulari.

"Vishukani" is a collection of many prosperous things such as grains, vegetables(cucumber, tender mango, jackfruit), fruits, lamp (Nilavilakku), Konna flowers, coconut, gold, mirror, Ramayana or Bhagavad-Gita (Hindu holy books) etc. are arranged in a huge uruli (a circular plate made of panchaloham - five metals) with the picture of Lord Krishna in the puja room. The arrangement of the Vishukani is finished with huge care in the previous evening by the lady of the house.

"Vishu pulari" (dawn of Vishu day) is a ritual to wake up very early morning and go to puja room with the eyes closed so that the first thing a person looks is the divine darshan of God with Vishukani. This ritual is noted as "Kanikanal". It is considered that at Vishu pulari (dawn of the prosperous Vishu day) one should watch the Vishukani have affluent, successful and peaceful year ahead.

"Vishukaineetam" is also a ritual in which head of the family or elder people distributed coin to children or younger or servants and other workers to wish them good fortune or luck. On this day some people provide Vishukaineetam as notes, on behalf of coins. It is really pleasant to watch each other how much each one has got a collection of Vishukaineetam amount.

Behind all these Vishu celebration is unfinished withou tcrackers and Vishu Sadya exists of vishu katta / vishu kanji prepared with rice, milk and coconut and other delicacies prepared with jack fruit, mango, kalan etc.

Thrissur Pooram

Thrissur Pooram is one of the wonderful and vibrant temple

festivals of Kerala celebrated in the Malayalam month of Medam, which generally comes in April or May. It is a time for the two traditional groups "Paramekkavu" and "Thiruvambadi" to present or show their majesty or grandiosity by contesting or challenging with each other in terms of the clothed elephants and umbrellas.

On the day before the closing of the Pooram the groups get in the Vadakumnatha temple through the western gate and come out through the southern gate to parade and had face to face. No wonder clothed or dressed elephants and the exchange of umbrellas, glowing or astonishing fireworks that continue till the dawn of the next finished day, alluring and appealing music of Panchavadyam (a combination of five percussion and wind instruments) and much more are really beautiful, stunning and mesmerizing. The prominent places that are noted for grand Pooram celebrations are as follow: Arattupuzha, Uthralikavu, Cheeram Kulangara, Thrissur, Mannarkkad, Perumanam, Pariyanampetta, Aryankavu, Mangottu, Kodikal, Medamkulangara and Thirumandhamkunnu. But the traditional groups that represent the major elements of Thrissur Pooram are Paramekkavu and Thiruvambadi.

Aranmula Snake Boat Race

Aranmula Boat Race is one of the divine or enjoyable religious fairsheld annually, usually during Septemberon Pampa River in Kuttanad region at Aranmula. This fair includes 30-40 snake boats (snake boats are named because of their shape rather than the living snake) racing against each other on Pampa River against the scenery of the 1,700-year-old Aranmula temple devoted to Sree Parthasarathy (the epitome of Lord Krishna in the form of Arjuna's charioteer),traditionally dressed rowers come along by groups of 25 singers are really amazing and mesmerizing. No wonder thousand of on lookers position themselves on the banks of the Pampa River near the temple in Aranmula for witness the wonderful or remarkable event.

Nehru Trophy Boat Race

Nehru Trophy Boat Race" noted as the largest snake boat race in the world held every year on the second Saturday of

August at Punnamada Lake near Alleppey is one of the most competitive and famous boat race in "God's Own Country" and no wonder it is the best time to book Alleppey Tour Packages.

Excluded from the snake boats with 100 to 120 rowers who dig or turn the water to the melody of the famous songs, there are many exclusive features of this event like ritual or formal water procession, wonderful water floats, decorated boats, vanchipattu, races of smaller country crafts, chundanvellom race which enthrall thousands of tourists to visit Alleppey and overwhelmed with an amazing treat.

10

Education

EDUCATION IN KERALA

The importance and antiquity of education in Kerala is underscored by the state's ranking as among the most literate in the country. The local dynastic precursors of modern-day Kerala - primarily the Travancore Royal Family, the Christian missionaries, The Nair Service Society, Sree Narayana Dharma Paripalana Yogam (SNDP Yogam) and Muslim Educational Society (MES) - made significant contributions to the progress on education in Kerala. There were many *sabha mathams* that imparted Vedic knowledge. Apart from *kalaris*, which taught martial arts, there were village schools run by Ezhuthachans or Asans. Christian missionaries brought the modern school education system to Kerala.

Education in Kerala had been promoted during British rule in India by Christian missionaries who were keen on providing education to all sections of society and on strengthening of women, without any kind of discrimination. The contributions of Catholic priests and nuns has been crucial and has played a major role in the education of women and members of lower strata of society, resulting in the surpassing of many social hurdles. A significant figure in the 19th century was Rev.fr. Kuriakose Elias Chavara, who started a system called "A school along with every church" to make education available for both poor and rich.

The University of Kerala's administrative building in Thiruvananthapuram

That system still continues in the present. His work has resulted in the promotion of education for girls and has become a model for the educational system in Kerala after independence. Kerala's high literacy rate is attributed to a high literacy rate among girls; as it is said, "When a woman is educated, she will make sure that her children are well-educated."

The Kerala school of astronomy and mathematics was founded by Madhava of Sangamagrama in Kerala, which included among its members: Parameshvara, Neelakanta Somayaji, Jyeshtadeva, Achyuta Pisharati, Melpathur Narayana Bhattathiri and Achyuta Panikkar. The school flourished between the 14th and 16th centuries and the original discoveries of the school seems to have ended with Narayana Bhattathiri (1559–1632). In attempting to solve astronomical problems, the Kerala school independently created a number of important mathematics concepts. Their most important results—series expansion for trigonometric functions—were described in Sanskrit verse in a book by Neelakanta called *Tantrasangraha*, and again in a commentary on this work, called *Tantrasangraha-vakhya*, of unknown authorship. The theorems were stated without proof, but proofs for the series for sine, cosine, and inverse tangent were provided a century later in the work Yuktibhâc□ (c.1500-1610), written in Malayalam, by Jyesthadeva, and also in a commentary on Tantrasangraha.

Their work, completed two centuries before the invention of calculus in Europe, provided what is now considered the first example of a power series (apart from geometric series). However, they did not formulate a systematic theory of differentiation and integration, nor is there any direct evidence of their results being transmitted outside Kerala.

Education

The University of Kerala in Thiruvananthapuram

The Kerala school of astronomy and mathematics flourished between the 14th and 16th centuries. In attempting to solve astronomical problems, the Kerala school independently created a number of important mathematics concepts, including series expansion for trigonometric functions. Following the instructions of the Wood's despatch of 1854, both the princely states, Travancore and Cochin, launched mass education drives with support from agencies, mainly based on castes and communities and introduced a system of grant-in-aid to attract more private initiatives. The efforts by leaders, Vaikunda Swami, Narayana Guru, Ayyankali and Kuriakose Elias Chavaratowards aiding the socially discriminated castes in the state, with the help of community-based organisations like Nair Service Society, SNDP, Muslim Mahajana Sabha, Yoga Kshema Sabha (of Nambudiris) and congregations of Christian churches, led to the development of mass education in Kerala.

Hardware training for students given by "IT@SCHOOL" project

In 1991, Kerala became the first state in India to be recognised as a completely literate state, though the effective literacy rate at that time was only 90%. As of 2007, the net enrolment in elementary education was almost 100% and was almost balanced among sexes, social groups and regions, unlike other states in India. The state topped the Education Development Index (EDI) among 21 major states in India in the year 2006–2007. According to the first Economic Census, conducted in 1977, 99.7% of the villages in Kerala had a primary school within 2 kilometres (1.2

mi), 98.6% had a middle school within 2 kilometres (1.2 mi) and 96.7% had a high school or higher secondary school within 5 kilometres (3.1 mi). According to the 2011 census, Kerala has 93.91% literacy compared to the national literacy rate of 74.04%. In January 2016, Kerala became the first Indian state to achieve 100% primary education through its literacy programme Athulyam.

The educational system prevailing in the state's schools is made up of 10 years, which are streamlined into lower primary, upper primary and secondary school stages with a *4+3+3* pattern. After 10 years of schooling, students typically enroll in Higher Secondary Schooling in one of the three major streams—liberal arts, commerce or science. Upon completing the required coursework, students can enroll in general or professional under-graduate (UG) programmes. The majority of public schools are affiliated with the Kerala State Education Board. Other educational boards are the Indian Certificate of Secondary Education (ICSE), the Central Board for Secondary Education(CBSE), and the National Institute of Open Schooling (NIOS). English is the language of instruction in most self-financing schools, while government and government-aided schools offer English or Malayalam. Though the cost of education is generally considered low in Kerala, according to the 61st round of the National Sample Survey (2004–2005), per capita spending on education by the rural households was reported to be 41 (57¢ US) for Kerala, more than twice the national average. The survey also revealed that the rural-urban difference in household expenditure on education was much less in Kerala than in the rest of India.

Present

Schools and colleges are mostly run by the government, private trusts, or individuals. Each school is affiliated with either the Indian Certificate of Secondary Education (ICSE), the Central Board for Secondary Education (CBSE), Kerala State Education Board or the (NIOS). English is the language of instruction in most private schools, while government run schools offer English or Malayalam as the medium of instruction. Government run schools in the districts bordering Karnataka and Tamil Nadu also offer instruction in Kannada or Tamil languages. A handful of Government Sanskrit Schools provide instruction in Sanskrit supplemented by Malayalam, English, Tamil or Kannada. After 10 years of secondary schooling, students typically enroll at Higher Secondary School in one of the three streams—liberal arts, commerce or science. Upon completing the required coursework, students can enroll in general or professional degree programmes. Kerala topped the Education Development Index (EDI) among 21 major states in India in year 2006-2007. In January 2016, Kerala became the 1st Indian state to achieve 100% primary education through its literacy programme Athulyam.

Quality of education

In spite of the large number of educational institutions in the state, the quality of education at all levels in Kerala has been showing a decline due to financial constraints resulting from quantitative expansion of the sector.

A study published in 1999 by the Centre for Socio-economic & Environmental Studies states that while the dropout rates are very low in primary schools, the same increases in the ninth and the tenth standards in Kerala. This is particularly true of SC/ ST students. Schools showed that only 73% of the students joining at 1st Standard reach the 10th Standard. In the case of scheduled caste students, only 59% reach the 10th standard. 60% of Scheduled Tribe students drop out by the 10th standard.

Another major indicator of the inefficiency of Kerala's school education system is the large-scale failure of the students in the matriculation examination. Only about 50% of the students who appear for the examination get through. The percentage has been considerably increased because of major interventions by the government in the areas of curriculum and teacher training. In March 2011, 91.37% students qualified for higher studies in the matriculation Examination.The grades in SSLC examination plays an important role in the admission procedure to colleges in Kerala.

Organisation

The schools and colleges in Kerala are run by the government or private trusts and individuals. Each school is affiliated with either the Indian Certificate of Secondary Education(ICSE), the Central Board for Secondary Education (CBSE), Kerala State Education Board or the National Institute of Open Schooling (NIOS). English is the language of instruction in most private schools, but government run schools offer both English and Malayalam as medium. After 10 years of secondary schooling, students typically enroll at Higher Secondary School in one of the three streams—liberal arts, commerce or science. Upon completing the required coursework, students can enroll in general or professional degree programmes. Lots of civil service institutes are there.

School Arts Festival in Palakkad

By region

Thiruvananthapuram

Thiruvananthapuram, the state's major academic hub, University of Kerala and several professional education colleges, including 15 engineering colleges, three medical colleges, three

Ayurveda colleges, two colleges of homeopathy, six other medical colleges, and several law colleges. Trivandrum Medical College, Kerala's premier health institute, one of the finest in the country, is being upgraded to the status of an All India Institute of Medical Sciences (AIIMS). The College of Engineering, Trivandrum is one of the prominent engineering institutions in the state. The Asian School of Business and IIITM-K are two of the other premier management study institutions in the city, both situated inside Technopark. The Indian Institute of Space Science and Technology, first of its kind in India, is also situated here and an Indian Institute of Science Education and Research, Thiruvananthapuram is also being set up.Trivandrum district holds the most number of colleges and schools in Kerala including 4 international schools, 30 professional colleges, and 38 vocational training institutes

Thiruvananthapuram is also home to most number of Research Centres in Kerala including ISRO, IISER, BrahMos Aerospace Private Limited, Vikram Sarabhai Space Centre(VSSC), Liquid Propulsion Systems Centre (LPSC), Thumba Equatorial Rocket Launching Station (TERLS) etc. The College of Engineering, Trivandrum is one of the prominent engineering institutions in the country. The Asian School of Business and IIITM-K are two of the other premier management study institutions in the city, both situated inside Technopark. The Indian Institute of Space Technology, the unique and first of its kind in India, is situated in the state capital.

Science and technology centres in Trivandrum

Thiruvananthapuram is a Research and Development hub in the fields of space science, information technology, bio-technology, and medicine. It is home to the Indian Institute of Science Education and Research, Vikram Sarabhai Space Centre (VSSC), Liquid Propulsion Systems Centre (LPSC), Thumba Equatorial Rocket Launching Station (TERLS), Indian Institute of Space Science and Technology (IIST), Rajiv Gandhi Centre for Biotechnology (RGCB), Tropical Botanical Garden and Research Institute, ER&DC – CDAC, CSIR – National Institute of Interdisciplinary Science and Technology, Free Software Foundation of India (FSFI), Regional Cancer Centre (RCC), Sree

Chitra Thirunal Institute of Medical Sciences and Technology (SCTIMST), Centre for Earth Science Studies (CESS), Central Tuber Crops Research Institute (CTCRI), Priyadarsini Planetarium, The Oriental Research Institute & Manuscripts Library, Chief Disease Investigation Office(CDIO) Palode, Kerala Highway Research Institute, Kerala Fisheries Research Institute, etc. A scientific institution named National centre for molecular materials, for the research and development of biomedical devices and space electronics is to be established in Thiruvananthapuram.College of Architecture Trivandrum(CAT), which specialise only on the architecture course, is another institution proposed to set up in the suburbs of the city.

Kochi / Ernakulam

Kochi is another major educational hub. The Cochin University of Science and Technology (also known as "Cochin University") is situated in the suburb of the city. Most of the city's colleges offering tertiary education are affiliated to the Mahatma Gandhi University. Other national educational institutes in Kochi include the Central Institute of Fisheries Nautical and Engineering Training, the National University of Advanced Legal Studies, the National Institute of Oceanography, Central Institute of Fisheries Technology and the Central Marine Fisheries Research Institute. College of Fisheries affiliated to Kerala Agricultural University is situated at Panangad, a suburban area of the city. Pothanicad, a village in Ernakulam district is the first panchayath in India that achieved 100% literacy. Sree Sankaracharya University of Sanskrit (SSUS), also famous as Sanskrit University, is situated in Kalady, in the Northern side of Ernakulam District.

Kozhikode

Kozhikode is the major education city in Kerala which is home to two of the premier educational institutions in the country; the IIMK, one of the thirteen Indian Institutes of Management, and the only National Institute of Technology in Kerala, the NITC. Other important educational institutions in the district include Calicut Medical College, Government Law College, Calicut, Government Engineering College Kozhikode,

College Of Applied Science IHRD, Kiliyand Kozhikode, College of Nursing Calicut, Kerala School of Mathematics, Govt. Dental College, Co-Operative Institute of Technology and Govt. Polytechnic College.

Malappuram

The progress that Malappuram district has achieved in the field of education during the last decade is tremendous. Great strides have been made in the field of female education. Malappuram district is home to three universities (University of Calicut, Aligarh Muslim University campus and Thunchaththu Ezhuthachan Malayalam University. And the state Government has proposed to establish two new universities, Ayurveda University and English and Foreign Languages University campus here.

The district also hosts a substantial amount of religious educational institutions such as Darul Huda Islamic University, which has more than 30 affiliated colleges throughout Kerala.

Bibliography

Copland, Ian: *The Princes of India in the Endgame of Empire, 1917–1947*, Cambridge, England: Cambridge University Press, 1997.

Dales, G. F.: *Ancient Cities of the Indus*, New Delhi, Vikas Publishing House PVT LTD., 1979.

Das, Kamal Kishore: *Economic History of Moghul India: An Annotated Bibliography, 1526-1875*. Calcutta: Santiniketan, 1991.

De Bary: *Self and Society in Ming Thought*, Columbia University Press, New York, 1970.

Duboi, Abbe: *Hindu Manners, Customs and Ceremonies*, Fifth Indian Impression, CUP, 1985.

Dumont, Louis: *The Caste System and Its Implications*, London, Granada Pub. Ltd., 1970.

Ernst, Carl : *The Shambhala Guide to Sufism*, HarperOne, 1999.

Frankel, Francine: *India's Political Economy, 1947-1977: The Gradual Revolution*, Princeton, Princeton University Press, 1978.

Gommans, Jos: *Mughal Warfare: Indian Frontiers and High Road to Empire 1500-1700*. London, 2002.

Guha, Sumit: *The Agrarian Economy of the Bombay Deccan, 1818-1941*, Delhi, Oxford University Press, 1985.

Habib, Irfan: *The Agrarian System of Mughal India, 1556-1707*. New York: Asia, 1963.

Harlan, Lindsey : *Religion and Rajput Women: The Ethic of Protection in Contemporary Narratives.*, University of California Press, 1992.

Heather Elgood : *Hinduism and the Religious Arts,* Cassell, NY, 2000.

Heimann, Betty: *Facets of Indian Thought*, Geroge Allen & Unwin, London, 1964.

Hopkins, Thomas J.: *The Hindu Religious Tradition*. Encino, California: Dickenson, 1971.

Hopkirk, Peter: *The Great Game: The Struggle for Empire in Central Asia*, Kodansha, 1992.

Hunter, W.W.: *The Indian Empire, Its People, History and Products*, London: Trubner & Co, Ludgate Hill, 1886.

Ira Mervin Lapidus, *Muslim Cities in the Later Middle Ages*, Cambridge, Mass, 1967.

Ishtiaq Hussian: *Administration of the Sultanate of Delhi*, New Delhi, 1971.

Ishwari Prasad: *History of Medieval India*, Allahabad, 1940.

Jane R.: *A Peaceful Realm: The Rise and Fall of the Indus Civilization*, Boulder, Colorado: Westview, 2001.

Jonathan M.: *Ancient cities of the Indus Civilization*, New York: Oxford University Press, 1998.

Kaviraj, G.: *Aspects of Indian Thought*, University of Burdwan, Calcutta, 1966.

Khan, Rana Muhammad Sarwar : *The Rajputs: History, Clans, Culture and Nobility*, Eastern Book Corporation 2005.

Khilnani, N. M.: *British Power in the Punjab 1839-1858*. New York, 1972.

Kishore, Kamal: *Economic History of Moghul India: An Annotated Bibliography, 1526-1875*. Calcutta: Santiniketan, 1991.

Lai, K.S., *History of the Khaljis*, Asia Publishing House, Bombay, 1967.

Marvin Lapidus: *Muslim Cities in the Later Middle Ages*, Cambridge, Mass., 1967.

Monica Juneja : *Architecture in Medieval India : Forms Contexts Histories*, Permanent Black, 2008.

Munni Pareek : *Early Indian Residential Architecture*, Harman Publishing, 2002.

Owen, Sidney J. : *The Fall of the Moghul Empire*, London, 1912,

Prasad Tiwari: *Foundations of Ancient Indian Culture*, Pointer Publishers, Delhi, 2001.

Ramusack, Barbara N.: *The Princes of India in the Twilight of Empire*, Ohio State University Press, 1978.

Sushil Kumar: *Ancient Indian Erotics and Erotic Literature*, Firma K. L. Mukhopadhyay, Calcutta, 1959.

Tahsildar Singh: *Architecture of North Indian Temples : C-400-1000 A.D.*, Jnanada Prakashan, Delhi, 2008.

Walter A. : *The Roots of Ancient India: The Archaeology of Early Indian Civilization*, New York: Macmillan, 1971.

Index

www.ingramcontent.com/pod-product-compliance
Ingram Content Group UK Ltd.
Pitfield, Milton Keynes, MK11 3LW, UK
UKHW042015290726
14061UKWH00001BB/14

9 789388 318785